CRIMINAL

The Trials of a New Jersey Criminal Defense Attorney

John W. Hartmann

D0067296

Plexus Publishing, Inc.
Medford, New Jersey

First Printing, 2012

Jacket: The Trials of a New Jersey Criminal Defense Attorney

Copyright © 2012 by John W. Hartmann

Published by:
Plexus Publishing Inc.
143 Old Marlton Pike
Medford, NJ 08055

Library of Congress Cataloging-in-Publication Data

Hartmann, John W., 1967-
The trials of a New Jersey criminal defense attorney / John W. Hartmann.
pages cm.
ISBN: 978-0-937548-75-2
1. Hartmann, Johyn W., 1967- 2. Criminial defense lawyers--New Jersey--Biography. I. Title.
KF373.H375A3 2012
345.0092--dc23
[B]

2012030468

Printed and bound in the United States of America.

President and CEO: Thomas H. Hogan, Sr.
Editor-in-Chief and Publisher: John B. Bryans
VP Graphics and Production: M. Heide Dengler
Managing Editor: Amy M. Reeve
Editorial Assistant: Brandi Scardilli
Cover Designer: Denise Erickson
Copyeditor: Beverly Michaels
Proofreader: Sheryl McGrotty
Marketing Coordinator: Robert Colding

www.plexuspublishing.com

To Marjule.
Now you know what
I'm doing all day.

PRAISE FOR *JACKET*

"Perfectly captures the rough and tumble world of a New Jersey
criminal defense attorney."
  —Robert Ramsey, author, *New Jersey Criminal Trial Objections*

"*Jacket* is an accurate portrait of the criminal justice system in NJ
and a rare treat for fans of true crime drama everywhere."
  —Jeffrey Evan Gold, legal analyst
  for Fox News, HLN, and Tru-TV

"Surprisingly honest and consistently entertaining."
  —Thomas J. Buck, Esq.

"A candid, colorful, and penetrating exposé of the gritty realities in
our criminal justice system. As a criminal defense lawyer raised in
New Jersey, I strongly recommend it."
  —Thomas Mesereau, the lawyer who acquitted Michael Jackson

"This book will change your life—especially if you're charged
with knocking over a liquor store in the Garden State. Hartmann
hits the perfect combination of trial strategy and personal anec-
dotes that makes for a great read."
  —Raymond Raya, attorney for Nicole "Snooki" Polizzi

"John Hartmann paints a vivid picture of the 'New Jersey Way' of
prosecuting and defending persons accused of crimes. ... *Jacket*
is a raucous ride through the New Jersey criminal court system."
  —Robert P. George, McCormick Professor
  of Jurisprudence, Princeton University

"Forget jurisprudence ... this is Jerseyprudence!"
  —Joanna M. Perilli, Esq.

CONTENTS

ACKNOWLEDGMENTS vii

Chapter 1   NATHANIEL 1

Chapter 2   THE WORKHOUSE 17

Chapter 3   HUSTLING VOTES 31

Chapter 4   WHITE SHIRT 55

Chapter 5   BABALORISHA 75

Chapter 6   HAVE GUN, WILL TRAVEL 99

Chapter 7   THE JUNGLE 119

Chapter 8   THE DEVIL'S LEFT HAND 141

Chapter 9   TOOLS OF THE TRADE 155

Chapter 10   TEN GUILTY PEOPLE 177

ABOUT THE AUTHOR 205

ACKNOWLEDGMENTS

I wrote *Jacket* in the hope that one day, God willing, when I am an old man, sitting ignored at the dinner table on Thanksgiving, complaining about the government, the mashed potatoes, and how the heat isn't set high enough, my children can turn to their children and say, "You know, he wasn't always like this." So, Lilly and Robert, thank you for inspiring me.

Heartfelt thanks go out to my wife, Marjule. She always encouraged me in my writing. As a teacher and published author herself, her careful editing of my entire work was instrumental in turning raw ideas into a book. Her mastery of verb tense (which remains a mystery to me) was a life saver. Also, some of the best lines in the book are hers, but she made me promise not to say which ones.

My mother-in-law, Marjule Drury, also read my manuscript and loved it, except for the original ending. She told me that the ending was terrible and that I better change it. I did. The new ending is much better. So, thank you, Marjule. My father, John F. Hartmann, also reviewed and edited *Jacket*. Thanks, Dad. Attorneys Thomas J. Buck, Jeffrey Evan Gold, Sharon Mahn, Joanna M. Perilli, Raymond Raya, and Robert Ramsey were also generous in making time to read and endorse the book.

Tom Mesereau, whom I consider the finest criminal defense attorney in the country, has my deep appreciation. I wrote Mr. Mesereau out of the clear blue sky asking him to read *Jacket* and consider writing a blurb. To my surprise, he called me up to say he'd do it. Even better, he spoke with me about the Michael Jackson trial and offered some excellent tips for opening statements. What I hadn't known when I first reached out is that Tom is from—you got it—New Jersey! No wonder he's both a great lawyer and a great guy.

Other friends read the original manuscript and gave me suggestions, including Susan Eichner, Susan Chianese, Whitney Mokros, and Shriek Lakkaraju. Thank you for your time, encouragement, and input. Also, I wish to thank author Poonam Sharma for giving me advice on the business end of publishing. It was an eye opener.

I would be remiss if I didn't thank the people who made the stories in this book possible, the people whom I have represented over the years, my clients. Thank you so much. You have made my interesting, independent, and exciting career possible. You are (almost) all innocent in my book. I especially want to thank the client who wrote me the following (you know who you are) when I really needed a laugh: "I was lucky to have such an awesome extremely unprofessional smart attorney!" I took that as a compliment.

I wish to thank everyone at the Middlesex County and Mercer County public defender's offices. Over the years, both offices have had some of the finest criminal defense attorneys anywhere working for them, and I know all of you guys (lawyers and staff) are doing a great job.

Over my career, I have worked with many attorneys. I have shared office space with three: Roger Daley, William Anklowitz, and Robin Echevarria. I really enjoyed working with all of you, so thank you. In addition, I wish to mention one other attorney, Howard Teitelbaum—a superb lawyer, a better businessman, and an all-around *mensch*. Howard bought my first book and actually read it, and for over a decade, every time he saw me, he asked, "How is my favorite author doing and when is your next book coming out?" Well, here it is, Howard.

I am thankful to everyone who provided a blurb for the cover of *Jacket*, especially Professor Robert George, a man who would be on the United States Supreme Court if he weren't so smart.

Thanks to the great folks at Plexus Publishing, Inc. It's been so much fun meeting and working with you. This includes Grace DiFilippo in customer service; Heide Dengler, VP of graphics and production; Denise Erickson, cover designer (Heide and Denise, awesome cover!); Kara Jalkowski, book designer; Amy Reeve, managing editor in the book division; Brandi Scardilli, editorial assistant in the book division; and Rob Colding, marketing coordinator.

Finally, I wish to thank the editor-in-chief of the book division, John B. Bryans. J.B. is the reason *Jacket* is a book (so blame him). J.B. read the manuscript after it was dumped on his desk one winter morning, and despite his very busy schedule, he liked it enough to work on it. J.B. did a crack job in editing *Jacket* and was patient in fielding my continual litany of questions. And, finally, everything he promised he promptly delivered on, a rare occurrence in any profession. So, John B. Bryans, thank you!

1

NATHANIEL

"Big John, I need a favor."

"Oh, shit," I thought to myself.

On the other end of the line was Vern Hayes, the Mercer County Public Defender. The last time I had done Vern a favor, a judge almost held me in contempt, so I had sworn never again. When Vern wanted a favor, it was usually a problem client he was hoping to unload on some unsuspecting attorney. However, he caught me in a moment of weakness. It was a Friday, and I had had a very good week. Anyway, helping Vern was a two-way street—he was always good at giving something back, whether it was advice or help with an expert witness or maybe even a case.

"Sure, Vern," I responded against my better judgment, "what do you need?"

"There's a file ready for pickup—a case remanded by the appellate division. Three years ago the defendant was convicted of robbing a convenience store, but the appellate court overturned the conviction because the judge failed to tell the jury the law on identification. Now the case is back, and you'll be starting from scratch.

"John, the thing about it is," he continued, "I read the opinion and talked to his prior attorney, and I think this guy may be innocent. They locked him up right after the verdict, and he's spent three years in jail for nothing. Unbelievable—what a system."

"Innocent, no way," I responded in disbelief, for Vern had been around a long time and did not say such things lightly. "Vern, everyone says they're innocent. How many trials have you had where they were really innocent?"

"I don't know, but, hell, what do you care?" Vern responded with a slight laugh. "Come get the file and go see the guy. He's at the workhouse."

"No problem, boss, you know me—I'll walk him out the door after trial. And you're right, I don't care," I said with half-feigned overconfidence.

I went to pick up the file four days later. The Office of the Public Defender is in Trenton, a small city that rests uneasily on the banks of the Delaware River in central New Jersey. The city was founded on its precise location because it was the farthest point north on the Delaware where large sailing ships could travel up river. Trenton became famous in 1776, when George Washington won a battle there on the day after Christmas, and a week later won another. After that, it slowly grew into an industrial center fed by immigrants from all over Europe, including Poles, Italians, Germans, and Jews. They were followed by a large influx of African Americans, mostly hailing from North Carolina, in their flight from Jim Crow. The Roebling factories gave the city a firm industrial base, and the metal coils that were used to construct the Brooklyn Bridge were forged in the fires of Trenton kilns. There was a reason why the iconic railroad bridge spanning the Delaware River from Trenton to Pennsylvania boasted in large, proud, illuminated letters: "Trenton Makes, The World Takes."

The riots of 1968 hit the city hard. You can still talk to people who remember the violence vividly, who remember having to be driven to work in the city by family members with a shotgun in tow and a German shepherd in the back. The riots were focused on an area in the center of the city near the State Capitol called the Battle

Monument, the spot where Alexander Hamilton had placed the cannons that were employed to blast the Hessians into submission during the Battle of Trenton. If you mention the Battle Monument today, the first thing that comes to mind is not the Revolutionary War but a particularly rundown section of the town that is rich in liquor stores and drug dealing, but little else.

After the riots, Trenton went into a steady decline. The last factories chained their gates shut in the early 1970s. Residents began leaving the city in droves, headed for the burgeoning suburbs as jobs disappeared, crime increased, and schools started to fail.

This is not to say that the city is lost. Unlike other urban areas in New Jersey, Trenton has an advantage: It is the state capital, and because big government is a way of life in New Jersey, there will always be a large employer located in the city. Therefore, while the city will never be in as desperate a condition as a place like Camden, for the eighty thousand or so residents who call Trenton home, their city's best days are behind it.

Conveniently situated on South Broad Street, the public defender's office is directly across from the Old Mercer County Courthouse, where the criminal courts are located. The courthouse itself is approximately a century old, and the spot has been home to judicial proceedings for over 180 years. In fact, Daniel Webster (whose street name was "Black Dan") argued a case there back in 1836. The adjective "old" aptly describes the place—it is a dump.

A couple of years ago the building had to be closed down because of mold infestation. A year after the mold attack, a janitor somehow fell into a gaping maw that had opened up in the main stairway and was sucked into the marble quicksand. So he was stuck, half suspended, between the flight of stairs and some unknown subterranean dungeon that held who knew what. After about three hours, when it was touch or go whether the poor soul would disappear forever into the bowels of the courthouse, he was rescued by a small army of Trenton firemen. He went from his dangling near-death experience right down Broad Street and limped into a personal injury lawyer's office, and he hasn't worked since.

To this day, large irregular stains mysteriously appear on courtroom ceilings and then disappear, like a toxic aurora borealis. The Old Mercer County Courthouse is little more than a brick and mortar carcinogen.

But at least the old courthouse has its charm. Whoever designed the *new* courthouse must have been on the take. This courthouse, where the civil and family parts are located, is a model of inefficiency. It has no readily accessible stairs. Its five floors are serviced by two teeth-grindingly slow elevators, one of which is invariably out of service. If you have a matter on any floor but the first, you had better be 10 minutes early or you run a serious risk of being late.

I entered the public defender's office that early afternoon and passed by the security officer, who never bothered me—presumably because I wore a suit and moved with a sense of purpose. Taking an elevator to the second floor, I greeted the secretary, who sat protected behind a wall with a large window, and was then buzzed into the office. Immediately to my left was the conference room. It was lunchtime, and a few public defenders I knew were in the room sitting at the large rectangular table, eating sandwiches and munching on chips. I knew and liked them all. I was in no rush so I stopped in to say hi. They were talking shop.

My friend Ed was reciting a familiar litany of woe. "I was in court today representing this guy who has two priors for distribution. He was nabbed with two bundles of heroin and $1,304 on him. The original offer was ten with a four. I convince the prosecutor to give him probation as long as he gets into a long-term inpatient drug program. Not only does the idiot not take it, he tells me I am trying to sell him out and if only he had a 'real' attorney and not a 'public pretender' he would get off. We go before the judge and he informs the court that I am not working on his behalf and that he is hiring somebody else. He then mentions he is talking to probably the worst attorney down here. Next he tells the judge that I won't listen to him and that I don't believe him when he says he is innocent. Hey, I guess the cops planted the drugs, the hand-to-hand was actually him doing a bump with his cousin, and the thirteen hundred in assorted bills was for rent—even though he was popped on the 20th and rent is due on the first. Yeah, a jury is going to buy that. The judge then let him have it, telling him you have an excellent attorney and you better think about that offer, and he adjourned the case for one week."

I've heard this conversation a million times. It's funny—public defenders are often the best lawyers in the courthouse, but because people don't pay them they assume they aren't any good. And so the accused will can an experienced public defender who has tried a hundred cases and enjoys a good working relationship with the prosecutor and the judge, and hire someone who has a nice office and a great webpage but wouldn't recognize a Fourth Amendment issue if it fell on his head and landed in his lap.

I sat down, made myself comfortable, grabbed the well-read sports page from a local paper haphazardly tossed on the table, and joined in the banter. There were the usual complaints about pain-in-the-neck prosecutors, pain-in-the-ass clients, and getting screwed by a judge in some ruling. Finally, somebody asked me what I was doing at the office.

"Picking up a file. Vern asked me to do him a favor."

Everyone laughed in unison. A lawyer named Chris said, "Weren't you held in contempt the last time you did a favor for Vern?" I responded that, no, I was *almost* held in contempt but not actually held in contempt. All of a sudden, I regretted my decision to take the case. At that point, lunch was over and most of my *compadres* had to go back to court. We said goodbye and I sauntered to the bin where the files ready for pickup are stored.

The solitary file was sitting there in the bin. Written in green letters on the front was the name *Nathaniel Smith*. Right away, it looked different from the typical file; most are thin, with almost nothing in them. They are also new. This file, Nathaniel Smith's file, was bulky. You could tell it was filled with police reports, transcripts, briefs, and an opinion. It had that characteristically worn, musty look of a file back on appeal. I picked it up with both hands and headed for the exit. I had done so many cases that I was usually in no rush to read the files. But Vern said he thought this man was actually innocent, and I was intrigued in spite of having told Vern I didn't care.

At this point, you may be wondering why a private attorney would be representing an indigent client. The reason is as follows: The public defender's office is a law office. Therefore, such issues as conflicts of interest apply to them as they would to regular law firms. Just as two attorneys from the same office usually cannot represent co-defendants, the public defender's office can also be conflicted out of cases. As a result, cases are "pooled" out to attorneys who are qualified and have requested to be placed on the pool list. When I started doing pool work in the mid-90s, it paid peanuts. It was now up to $50 an hour out of court and $60 an hour in court. I had stopped doing pool work in bulk a couple of years earlier because my practice was going pretty well, but I always liked to have a few pool cases going at any particular time. As I said, Vern was always good in returning a favor.

I returned to my car and drove the seven miles back to my office. I had hung my shingle in a section of West Windsor, the town where I grew up, called Princeton Junction. The Junction is located within walking distance of a railroad station where you can hop a train that will get you to Newark in 45 minutes and to New York City in a little over an hour. My office is on the second floor of a rundown building. The only way to access the second floor is via the longest uninterrupted flight of stairs you have ever seen—20 steps going straight up. I have no idea how it made code. Some of the other tenants are a realtor, an investment adviser, and a tailor named Sal. Until recently, we also had two massage parlors, but the local police closed the one in the back and the FBI raided the one in the front. Needless to say, it's not the high-rent district, even though my landlord charges me as though it were.

My office is small, no frills. I have a small waiting room, a small conference room, and two small offices. I share the office with another attorney named Robin. In my career, I have shared office space with two other lawyers, and both of them are now judges. I am pretty certain the "robe streak" has come to end.

The rooms are admittedly not much to look at. There are a number of shelves in the conference room filled with legal books. It looks impressive, but in actuality the books are so out of date as to be almost useless. A few random pictures and my college degree break the monotony of the poorly painted walls. I don't physically have my law school diploma because I blew off the graduation ceremony and the provost wouldn't mail it to me. Hanging behind my "Staples Period" desk is a large poster of a cartoon caricature with suspicious eyes and a large nose peering over a wall. It reads "Just

because you are paranoid doesn't mean they are not out to get you."
When I am meeting with clients in my office, they sit in an interview chair facing the poster on the wall behind me. It provides a
not-so-subtle message.

A client once described my office ambiance as "underground,"
and I took it as a compliment. I like to keep things a little
unkempt—some dust on the table, files lying around, papers on the
conference table. It lends the appearance of a busy office. As an
analogy, consider this: You find yourself in a small town that you
have never visited before, and you need a haircut. You look in the
phone book, and there are two barbers in town. You go to the first
one, and it is a mess, hair all over the place. Then you head over to
the second barber, and the place is immaculate, nothing out of
place. Where do you go to get your haircut? You go to the first
establishment. It's a mess because that's where everyone in town
goes, and the townies know best. It's the same with my office; it
might not be the neatest, but you know when you walk in that a lot
of people have hired me. Presumably because I know what I'm
doing and get good results.

The other benefit of a small office is that it keeps the expenses
down. As a result, I can charge less than most other attorneys who
have larger offices and support staff. In the area of criminal law,
controlling your expenses is very important. Many of the clients we
represent are poor. So the secret to success in this business is to
offer people a competitive price and provide excellent service—or,
as a fellow attorney once said, "Reasonable doubt at a reasonable
price." Sure, you may lose the occasional wealthy client who looks
down his nose at you, but for every one of them there are 10 people
from working-class backgrounds who breathe a sigh of relief when
you tell them it is not going to cost them two weeks' salary to hire

you. In my line of work, every dollar you save is a dollar you earn, and my profit margin is well over 70 percent, which is great in almost any line of business.

I plopped Nathaniel Smith's file on the conference table with the intention of digging right in. But since it was two o'clock, the mail had already arrived, so I went through it first. It consisted mainly of court notices. I promptly hand-wrote the dates onto the "Weird New Jersey" calendar my wife had bought me for Christmas. There were letters from an attorney and a judge, and as these required immediate responses, I typed them out and put them in the outgoing mail tray. There was also a check for $500 from a client with whom I had worked out a payment plan.

By the time I'd finished with the mail and returned a few phone calls, I had lost over an hour but was finally able to walk the 10 feet from my desk to the head of the conference table where my new file lay. As I mentioned before, this file was thick. Taking it out of its jacket, I reviewed the first documents, the discovery from the case. The discovery consisted of a police report, an investigative report from a detective, a typed sworn statement from a witness, and a black-and-white copy of a photo lineup consisting of nine African American males. Photo lineups are taken in color, but because this was just a Xerox copy, the nine pictures seemed older than they were. The men's shadowy visages appeared eerie, like bygone photos you might see in a history textbook of men who were lynched in the 1920s. After reviewing the discovery, I skimmed the transcripts from the trial. Finally, I read the appellate court's decision that had reversed the jury's conviction and brought the case to my desk.

By the time I finished the final page of the decision, it was dark outside. I put the file back in its jacket, filled out a time sheet, placed the file in a cabinet, and prepared to head out to municipal court. As I turned out the lights and locked the office door behind me, I was thinking Vern might be right, that Nathaniel Smith probably *was* innocent and had been falsely convicted. Here was a 50-year-old man with no criminal record, who had been charged, indicted, convicted, and sent to jail, where he waited for three years for his appeal to be filed, briefed, argued, and eventually decided in his favor. Three years behind bars for nothing, absolutely nothing.

This is what I found out from reading the file: The robbery had occurred at a local food market called Halo Farms on Wednesday, November 17, at approximately 7:20 PM. At that time, an African American male entered the store. There were no customers in the market at that time, only two young women working the registers at the front, and a manager and another employee in the back. The individual grabbed a small item from dairy and then went to one of the registers. He placed the item on the conveyer belt with his left hand and pulled a knife out of his coat pocket with the right. He then looked at the cashier and demanded the money from the register. The woman complied, handing him approximately $310 in assorted bills, and the man left. From the time the robber approached the register to the time he exited the market was less than 30 seconds.

The cashier who had been robbed immediately told her co-worker at the neighboring cash register what had happened. That cashier in turn notified the manager, who called the police. An officer was on the scene in five minutes. He spoke with the 18-year-old African American cashier whose register had been robbed. Despite being visibly upset, she gave a description of the perpetrator: He was a middle-aged black male dressed in dark clothing. He wore a cap on his head and had slight facial hair. She estimated the robber was a few inches taller than she was, giving her own height as five foot seven. After she'd provided her initial statement and about 15 minutes after the robbery, the detective in charge showed up. Meanwhile, the first officer on the scene took a statement from the girl who'd been working the adjacent register. Her story was consistent with that of the victim, including her estimate of the robber's age and height; he probably stood a little less than six feet, she said. Six feet at most.

Halo Farms is located in the southernmost part of Lawrence Township in a heavily populated and traveled area of town. It's just a block from the Trenton city limits and about two blocks from the Ewing Township border, in the middle of a business district whose other notable establishments include a beauty salon, a car wash, two gas stations, assorted eateries including a McDonalds, and a strip joint. The business district is part of a racially mixed working-class neighborhood of 80-year-old row houses, meaning the robber would have blended into the surroundings within seconds of leaving the market. It seemed clear to me what had happened: Some junkie needed cash for his local drug dealer so he could get his hit. By the time the detective arrived on the scene, the perp was probably in an abandoned row house in Trenton, firing up his crack pipe with shaking hands.

It was at this point that my newest client Nathaniel Smith became caught up in the investigation. A summary of his statement to the police was in the detective's report, so I was able to quickly learn his side of the story.

Nathaniel worked two jobs. During the day he was a handyman, doing all sorts of odd jobs around his Trenton neighborhood; evenings he would walk from his house to a bus stop near Halo Farms and take a bus seven miles north to Princeton. There, he would transfer to another bus and ride an additional seven miles to

Montgomery Township, where he worked making phone calls for a telemarketing firm. On the evening of the robbery, Nathaniel had showed up at the bus stop early. He'd been helping a neighbor with a backed-up toilet late into the afternoon, after which he took a quick shower at home before heading to his night job. He stopped at a fast food restaurant and ordered a fish sandwich and a can of grape soda, then walked two blocks to the bus stop and sat down to eat his meal.

At about 7:45 PM, the detective walked out of the market and decided to drive around the area to look for the robber. A block or so away, sitting on the curb eating his sandwich and drinking his soda, he happened upon Nathaniel Smith. Nathaniel fit the general description of the robber as a middle-aged African American male with some facial hair, dressed in dark clothing. Of course, there were probably a dozen or more men who fit that description within a hundred-yard radius of the bus stop at the time.

The detective stopped the car, got out, and started to talk to Nathaniel before eventually asking him to stand up. Up stood a six foot four, rail-thin individual, at which point any suspicion of Nathaniel Smith as the suspect should have gone out the window. The cashier who'd been robbed had described the suspect as a few inches taller than she was, a statement corroborated by her co-worker. From their descriptions of a man who stood six feet or less, the detective should have realized he was barking up the wrong tree. Instead, he continued to question Nathaniel in a loud and insin-uating voice.

Nathaniel, exhausted from his day's work, not particularly look-ing forward to another six hours or so on the telemarketing job, and none too happy at being questioned aggressively by a policeman about events he had no knowledge of, began to yell back. At this point, the detective decided Nathaniel had something to hide and ordered him into the back of his car. As he drove back to Halo Farms, just a block away, he radioed ahead telling the police to bring the cashier outside to the curb.

What was conducted next is called a "show up." The witness was waiting outside the market when the police cruiser arrived with Nathaniel Smith scrunched up in the back seat. The detective got out of the car and told her he had a suspect in the back. He shone his flashlight into Nathaniel's face and the cashier said, after two seconds, "That's the guy."

The detective's job was now almost over. He handcuffed Nathaniel and drove him to the police station where he placed him in an interview room, read him his Miranda rights, and tried to take a statement. At first Nathaniel talked, but when it became clear the detective didn't care what his side of the story was and only wanted him to confess to the robbery, he asserted his right to speak with an attorney. The detective stopped the interview—he really didn't need a statement anyway—and had Nathaniel's mug shot taken, and he wrote out a charge sheet for first degree armed robbery, third degree terroristic threats, and third degree possession of a weapon.

After typing out the charges on a multi-copy form, the detective separated the copies and handed Nathaniel his charge sheet, also known as a "green sheet" for the color of the paper it's printed on. Next the municipal court judge was called to set bail. Bail is based on a number of factors but the greatest weight is placed upon the seriousness of the offense and a defendant's criminal record. First degree armed robbery is about as serious an offense as you can catch without a body, so even though Nathaniel had no criminal record, the judge did not go easy. Bail was set at $150,000 cash or bond.

It took a little over one hour for Nathaniel Smith to go from sitting quietly at a bus stop, eating a fish sandwich and sipping a grape soda, to finding himself on a one-way trip to the Mercer County Correction Center.

The next part of the investigation consisted of bringing the cashier who had been robbed to the station to be interviewed. While the young woman was en route in a police car, the detective prepared a photo lineup to show her. He took Nathaniel's photo and put it inside a cardboard jacket designed by the New Jersey State Police specifically for this procedure. After placing that photo in slot four, the detective and another officer scoured a database of arrestees to find pictures of eight other African American men who fit the same general description as the suspect. Because Nathaniel was much older than the average armed robbery suspect, this took a little longer than usual, but they eventually had nine shots in the photo array, including Nathaniel's.

The cashier arrived at the station, and the interview got underway. First the detective talked to her about the case, and then he instructed her regarding the photo lineup. In general, the instructions are that the suspect may or may not be in the lineup; that people's appearance, such as the style of their hair, may change; and that the witness is not to guess. At this point, the detective showed the photo lineup to the young woman. Almost immediately she pointed to number four, the picture of Nathaniel Smith. This identification was hardly surprising as the woman had so recently seen Nathaniel sitting in the back of the police car, a flashlight beam in his face. The detective next had her initial the space under Nathaniel's picture to memorialize her selection. Once this was done, he took a formal statement from the victim and then closed the case.

Another file off his desk, another man on his way to jail.

It should be clear to anyone reviewing the circumstances just described—with the unfortunate exception of the detective in charge—that a problem with this case is the height of the suspect. The victim never saw Nathaniel Smith standing up; she first encountered him sitting in the back of a police car, and she later saw only his photograph. She could not have known that Nathaniel would have towered over her had they stood next to one another. In her formal statement, she gave the same description of the perpetrator as she gave to the first responding police officer: The robber was a few inches taller than she was. The identification was certainly false. But it was too late; the detective had already made up his mind.

I continued perusing the file, moving on to the trial transcripts. Two things stood out. First was that the second cashier, a young woman who saw the perpetrator if not the actual crime, was not called as a witness by the defense. Second, Nathaniel had not testified. This struck me as peculiar because he had no criminal record. Criminal records can be used to impeach a witness, so if your client has one, you usually think twice about sticking him on the stand. However, if your client has no record, you will often, though not always, want to have him tell his side of the story. I needed to know why Nathaniel had not testified.

The trial was actually very straightforward, and the openings, testimony, and summations only lasted one day. After the jury was charged—that's when the judge reads them the law and instructions—they came back in about two hours with a guilty verdict. The case was subsequently overturned because the judge had forgotten to give the Green charge—a charge named for the case *State v. Green*, which mandates that certain instructions be given to the jury where identification is an issue. Because the Green charge is so basic and because Nathaniel's public defender was experienced and the judge was new to the criminal bench, I wondered if the attorney intentionally did not ask for it in order to create an issue for appeal. If that was how it happened, it was a great move by the defense. Trial attorneys will tell you that most jurors don't even listen to the jury charge, which usually lasts well over an hour, with some jurors nodding off as the judge reads the law in a monotonous tone.

As cases go, this one was weak for the State. Actually, it was incredibly, unbelievably weak. I couldn't believe the police charged Nathaniel Smith. I couldn't believe a grand jury indicted Nathaniel Smith. I couldn't believe the State wasted its time going to trial with this dog of a case, and I *sure* couldn't believe a jury convicted Nathaniel Smith. But here we were. This man had now done three years for a crime he almost certainly did not commit. And he would have had to do substantially more if the appellate court had not reversed the matter on what was little more than a technicality.

"This guy really *is* innocent," I thought to myself after reviewing the file, "and I have to defend him."

Talk about pressure.

2

THE WORKHOUSE

It was time to pay a visit to Nathaniel Smith at the Mercer County Correction Center.

The Mercer County Correction Center, also known as the Mercer County Workhouse, also known simply as "the county," is the local jail. The Mercer County Correction Center is not referred to as "The Big House" and is certainly not called "The Poky." If you refer to it by these antiquated names, correction officers, experienced lawyers, and inmates who have been "guests" at the facility will look at you like you have two heads.

In New Jersey, there are 21 counties. Each county is a separate government entity, which, among other government functions, has responsibility for running the courts. This responsibility includes housing inmates at a county jail, and so each county has its own jail. The standards for these jails vary. Among career criminals, it is generally recognized that the best New Jersey county jail to be housed in is Hunterdon County. The Hunterdon jail is small, clean, and well-run, and doesn't have a lot of inmates. Hell, *I* could "build time there," as some prisoners put it. From what I hear, the *worst* county jail in the state is the Passaic County Jail in Paterson.

Various types of inmates are housed in county correctional facilities. First, there are the defendants facing State charges, anywhere from drug raps to murder, who can't make bail. Aside from "going out feet first," one of two things can happen to them: They can receive a probationary sentence and eventually be released, or they can be sentenced to state prison. Those who receive a state prison sentence are moved from the county correction center into the state prison system and are no longer the county's concern.

In addition to defendants facing state prison sentences, there are a number of prisoners who are incarcerated at county for relatively minor matters. Some motor vehicle violations can result in jail, for instance, including multiple convictions for driving with a suspended license. Men, and even the occasional woman, who owe child support are locked up and have to wait in jail until they see a judge. There are also a large number of inmates arrested on warrants issued when they failed to appear in municipal court to answer for motor vehicle offenses and minor criminal charges.

It always amazes me how some people simply ignore their requirements to go to court. When they are trying to avoid jail time, I can understand their dilatory ways, but too many just blow court off. Or they may have gone to court, pled guilty, been fined, worked out a payment plan—and then simply not paid, rather than going back to court to explain their financial situation to the judge. They fail to appear or fail to make a payment, and so a warrant is issued and the court suspends their driver's license.

It always catches up with them. Typically, they're stopped by the cops while driving, a warrant search is run, and the next thing they know they're wearing cuffs in the back seat of a state trooper's Ford. And they always seem to get arrested on a Friday, which means they often can't bail out until Monday, thereby securing for themselves a wonderful weekend as guests of the Mercer County Workhouse. In many cases, they have warrants (also known as detainers) from other towns in the county, so if they cannot make bail they have to wait, sometimes for a week or even more, to talk to a judge. Some local courts have begun to talk to workhouse inmates via video, but in many cases, it still takes weeks to talk to the judge in order to work out a new payment plan or plead guilty and be released. An even bigger problem arises when they have detainers from other counties or even other states, often Bucks County, Pennsylvania, which is right across the Delaware River. Such a person might get stuck in jail for months, becoming a correctional nomad, transported from county to county while working out legal obligations that have accumulated over the years. It's shocking the number of people walking around with warrants and even more shocking that it doesn't seem to bother them. This is why prosecutors and defense attorneys joke that if it weren't for people doing stupid things, none of us would have jobs.

The Mercer County Workhouse is located in the rural part of the county (yes, there are rural areas in New Jersey) in Hopewell Township. You get there by taking a rather pleasant and historic drive up Route 29, a bucolic two-lane road that hugs the Delaware River. Route 29 runs along the Delaware Canal, which was built in the middle of the 19th century by Irish immigrants. Along the way is Washington Crossing State Park, where General Washington and the Continental Army landed after crossing the Delaware before the Battle of Trenton. As you continue north, you'll spot a large hill looming over the Pennsylvania side of the river, a stone tower resembling a medieval keep moored on its top. This edifice is Bowman's Hill Tower, a lookout built during the Revolutionary War. I've often driven this road in the late afternoon, and as the sun begins to set and the silhouette of the tower catches my eye, I have the sensation of being in the Scottish highlands, an ocean away from Trenton.

To get to the workhouse, you make a right off Route 29 and drive 200 or so yards up a hill to a large chain-link fence. At the bottom of the hill is the Mercer County Wildlife Center, as well as a large

abandoned mill of some sort. You arrive at the gate, where a corrections officer in a booth greets you. He takes a look at your driver's
license and attorney identification card and lets you into the parking
lot. Once you drive onto jail property, you may see one of the feral
cats that live on the grounds. There is a large family of felines that
have made the jail grounds its home. Nobody bothers them, and they
appear to be well fed, probably from the prisoners' leftovers. The
Tower of London has its ravens. The Rock of Gibraltar has its monkeys. The Mercer County Workhouse has its cats.

Visiting the workhouse is a bit of an art. You have to know the
best time to arrive. During the day, there are shift changes, prisoner
counts, and meals served. In theory, an attorney can visit his client
whenever he wants, but in reality, if you don't want to spend three
hours locked down in the visiting area, twiddling your thumbs with
nothing to do, you have to know how to time the visit. I like to arrive
right at 4:00 PM. Shift change is at 3:00 PM., followed by a count that
lasts one hour. At 4:00 PM, you still have an hour before dinner is
served. Also, it is generally less hectic at this time of day, with fewer
people, such as members of the parole board, coming to visit. At
most, you may have another attorney or a bail bondsman. The officers who work the evening shift also tend to be more laid back.

After you park, you walk across the parking lot to a ramp that
leads into the main pedestrian entrance. This area is the older section of the jail, built in the 1960s. The section attached to it was
constructed about 25 years ago. Overall, it's a rundown facility. The
inmates are housed in a number of separate units called "pods,"
which are mostly identified by letters of the alphabet. Which pod
you're sent to depends on a number of factors. If you are serving a
short sentence, you will be placed in one pod. If you are in protective custody, you will be placed in another pod. If you have been

identified as belonging to a gang, usually by your tattoos, you will be placed in yet another pod. If you are charged with a serious offense and have a high bail, you will probably find yourself in A or B pod, located on the lower level of the jail.

All inmates wear the same type of clothing—in Mercer County, an orange jumpsuit with the large letters *MCCC* printed on the back. The shoes inmates wear, also orange, are more like slippers. Only inmates' socks are not orange; they're white tube socks. Civilians visiting the workhouse are prohibited from wearing orange, and those who do are turned back at the gate. A few years ago the owner of a local clothing store came up with the bright idea of selling knock-off prison jumpsuits. The first customer to purchase and wear the orange faux prison garb was immediately picked up by police, who pegged him as an escapee from "the county." Despite his protestations that he was just trying to make a fashion statement, the young man spent a night in the Trenton lockup and the clothing line lost its bid to become the hit of the fashion season.

As with any other jail, the workhouse is not a pleasant place. It's overcrowded and has a gang problem. If there is a riot in one of the pods, guards will come in with industrial-sized mace cans attached to large hoses and spray the prisoners indiscriminately, like firemen putting out a five-alarm fire. Due to chronic underfunding, there are almost no social services provided to any of the inmates. The food is terrible. I have been told that half of the recruits who sign up to be corrections officers leave after their first day of training. Most lawyers hate visiting the place.

That said, I've never minded visiting the county correction facility. The security is tight, and it is fairly well run. Also, although it houses criminals, most of them are focused on minding their business and getting through what they have to get through. And I've learned that inmates are grateful for an attorney visit, because many will go for months without seeing their lawyer. If you want to practice criminal law, you have to be willing to go to a jail; if you do not, you will have no credibility with your client. Nothing is worse than seeing an inmate who is brought over to court, sitting in the "box" (slang for jury box), yelling at his attorney, justifiably, because he hasn't seen him and is now expected to make a decision on a plea he only heard about two minutes earlier. I made the decision at the beginning of my career never to be on the receiving end of such a tirade. In this line of work, you come to understand why one of the seven (and least emphasized) Corporal Works of Mercy is to visit the incarcerated. Anyone can throw a buck into the poor box in church on Sunday, but few of us are willing to go see people in jail.

When I mention the workhouse to acquaintances, I'm often asked, "Why do they call it the workhouse when there's so little work going on there?" This is a misconception, for there is actually quite a bit of work that the inmates do. Most inmates, excepting those facing very serious charges, have jobs such as cleaning the pods or other areas of the jail. They may work in the kitchens, cooking and serving food, and even baking. Some inmates are given road detail, which means they are taken in buses to public areas around Mercer County to clean up trash. Working the roads is a plum assignment; not only do you get out into the fresh air, but you earn $10 a day, which is placed on your commissary account. Under the circumstances, the administration does the best it can to try to keep everyone busy on the theory that the more inmates have to do, the less opportunity they have to get into trouble.

As always in a prison, there is an underground economy at which prisoners work very hard. I am continually amazed at the truly ingenious solutions to problems that they come up with. Take, for instance, the need for alcohol when none is readily available. The prisoner's solution to this problem is called "hooch," a horrendous jailhouse concoction that is, in the words of the inmate who told me how to make it, "banging-your-head-off-bars bad."

Here is the recipe for proper hooch:

First, take a large plastic container, approximately 6 inches high, 10 inches wide, and 12 inches long, and fill it with water. Next, take whatever fruit you can find, smash it up, and place it in the container. Sprinkle in two cups of sugar that you have accumulated over the weeks by saving what you are given with your morning coffee. Add seven slices of bread that you have rolled up into balls and place them in the jailhouse still. (This provides the yeast.) Seal the container and place it in a garbage bag.

It takes approximately two weeks from this point for fermentation to begin in earnest, though the time will vary depending on how rotten the fruit was when first placed in the container. You have now reached the most dangerous point in the process, for the devilish concoction is highly susceptible to detection by guards who will seize and destroy it, and by prisoners who need to get their drink on. A good strategy is to enlist three or four other inmates to help you move the trash bag around. In another two weeks, open and enjoy your Mercer County "firewater" and hope you live to see another day.

An even more ingenious example of how to work with what you have in prison is tattooing. I was talking to a client once in my office and noticed a tattoo on his right arm of wings with his mother's name on it. The conversation was starting to lag, so I said, "Hey, I like your tattoo." He responded, "Thanks, I got it in prison. Do you want to know how they did it?" Of course, my curiosity was aroused, and I responded in the affirmative.

The individual who tattooed my client took a cardboard commissary sheet (given to inmates to keep track of their prison store provisions) and placed toothpaste on one end. He wrapped the sheet around to form a cone, the toothpaste keeping it together. He then placed checker pieces—it didn't matter if they were red or black—at the bottom of his locker and set the cone above them. Next, he set the checker pieces on fire. After that he placed another commissary sheet on top of the cone. The burning checker pieces created soot that accumulated on the bottom of the overlying sheet.

The next step was to scrape the soot off the sheet. He mixed the soot with a makeshift antiseptic, either toothpaste or shampoo. This was the ink. A staple was sharpened on the concrete cell wall to a fine point, creating a needle. The tat artist then wrapped the needle in string and placed it in the body of a ball point pen (with the ink stick removed). The needle was then dipped in the "prison ink," and the tattooing began. The job cost my client three ramen noodle soup cups that he purchased from commissary.

Now, don't think that the jails are full of budding entrepreneurs. Unfortunately, many people are in jail because they are just not that bright. I once had a conversation with a young man that went something like this:

"You have got to get me out of here, man. I am about to become a father. My girlfriend is pregnant, and I've been in here 11 months already."

"Wait a second. You've been here 11 months?"

"Yes."

"And your girlfriend is pregnant?"

"Yes."

"And you are about to become a father?"

"Yes."

"Eh … Congratulations. I hope it works out for you."

We're not talking rocket scientists here.

***

On the day I first went to visit Nathaniel Smith at the workhouse, I checked in with an officer sitting at a desk and signed the log book. I handed him my attorney ID and the keys to my car. This is all standard procedure. Cell phones are strictly forbidden, and it is a crime to use a cell phone in any jail in New Jersey. You can only bring in your files and a note pad. Items such as books and newspapers are considered contraband and thus also forbidden. The officer gives you a numbered identification card that you attach to your clothing, usually your lapel if you are wearing a suit. (I'm not particularly superstitious, but the few times I was given the identification number "13" I gave it back and asked for another. The guards probably thought I was crazy, but why tempt fate?)

Once you've put on your ID card, the officer "wands" you with a handheld metal detector, then calls Master Control. A steel door is opened remotely, and as it closes behind you, another opens immediately ahead of you. You have now entered the jail. You go through another steel door and walk down a hall, passing the medical unit, the officers' dining hall, and another metal door with paper covering its window. This is the Internal Affairs office. Ahead on your left is what was originally the inmate dining hall but is now the area where, among other activities, attorneys meet with their clients. A guard is sitting there. You give him your name and the list of clients you want to see, and then you tell him which of eight cubicles you will be waiting in. Unless it's occupied, I always pick cubicle number four because it's the farthest away from the guard and provides the most privacy. You then sit and wait for your first client to be brought up.

On this day, I had two clients to see. First the guards brought me a client I'll call Diara. We discussed his robbery case, and he insisted that he wasn't involved. In fact, he had an alibi: He claimed he was with his girlfriend when the robbery went down. Who was I to say he wasn't telling the truth? I explained to him that I had interviewed his girlfriend and taken a statement from her, and I had filed a motion to dismiss the case because of the improper way it was presented to the grand jury. I handed him a copy of the papers. After 20 minutes, he seemed satisfied and we wrapped up our conversation. He stood to leave, and as he started walking away, he turned back to me and said, "Hey, Mr. Hartmann, I hear you are representing Mr. Nathaniel Smith."

I responded, "Yes, I am. News sure travels fast in here."

"Well, you know, Mr. Hartmann, he's innocent."

"That's what I hear, Diara. And by the way, you've also told me *you* are innocent."

Diara smiled and said, "I know I did, Mr. Hartmann, but this guy really *is* innocent. Everyone knows it. Have a nice day and thanks for coming up to see me. Don't forget to call my mom and tell her I'm okay."

"I will, Diara, as soon as I get out of here."

Nathaniel Smith was next on my list. I was already intrigued by his case, and Diara's comments had further piqued my interest. I was looking forward to meeting Nathaniel, and having spoken to the prosecutor that morning, I had some good news for him: In light of his having served three years in jail, and given the general weakness of the case and the fact that the detective who'd arrested him now worked for Homeland Security—makes me feel *so* safe—and would be difficult to bring back for another trial, the prosecution was willing to offer him time served. All he had to do was plead guilty to a theft charge, and he would be out in a matter of days. I could get him into court by the end of the week, and by the weekend, he could be watching the Eagles–Giants game with his family and friends, drinking a cold one. This was very good news, and I couldn't wait to share it with him.

And, yet, I couldn't just walk up to him and say, "Hi Mr. Smith, I'm your court-appointed attorney. Plead guilty and get out of jail." That would be bush league, and from what I'd learned already about my client, he would be hesitant about pleading guilty. Instead, I would talk about the case. I would explain the options and possible outcomes. I would promise to fight this thing to the bitter end if he wanted me to. On the other hand, he might plead willingly. Having been in this situation before, I knew that some clients—even those who have insisted on their innocence—will say *anything* for a ticket out of the Mercer County Correction Center. (Hell, some would admit to being the gunman on the Grassy Knoll if it would get them out of jail.) I had no idea what position Nathaniel Smith might take on this, but if necessary, I was ready to give him what defense attorneys call the "Come to Jesus" talk. I had given it a lot, I was good at it, and today I was going to bring it. If I ran into resistance, I had already thought of the ultimate closing line: "Hey, you can't fight the man. You gave it a shot and lost. You ate three years for nothing. You want justice? Well, wait until you die, because you sure aren't going to get it here."

If that sounds cynical, well maybe it is. On the other hand, unless you have spent three years in jail, or three days for that matter, you'd better not judge anyone's motives for copping a plea. Most people would rather field-test bombs than spend time in jail, and I expected Nathaniel to be no different. Furthermore, while the case against him was weak, he had been convicted once by a jury. They had heard the evidence and found him guilty, and from what I heard, they weren't even out that long. Maybe he really *was* guilty. In any case, if Nathaniel wanted to plead guilty to get out of jail, I wasn't going to stand in his way.

I sat in cubicle number four thinking about what I was going to say. My file and notes were spread out on the bolted-down table. Most lawyers sit facing the entrance of the cubicle, with their backs to the wall. Not me; I always sit with my back to the entrance, facing the wall. I do this for a reason. When I first started practicing, an experienced public defender told me never to allow a client to get between you and the exit. Some prisoners have serious mental issues, and though it is rare, clients may become violent after hearing bad news. If they start acting up, you want to be able to make a quick exit. I've never had to put this advice to the test, but I am grateful that it was given to me and I try to pass it along to other attorneys, especially women.

Nathaniel was brought to my cubicle. I stood up and shook his hand and introduced myself. I was immediately struck by how tall he was. I knew from the record that he stood six foot four, but in person he seemed even taller. He was thin as a rail. He sat down, and we started to talk. I briefly explained my qualifications and why I was representing him. He sat quietly, pensively, taking it all in. I soon realized that he was just a little different—I couldn't put my finger on it, but there was something refreshingly unusual about him. He comported himself with a certain dignity that is rarely found behind prison walls.

I reviewed the case with Nathaniel, and then he filled me in on his side of the story. I told him what I thought of his previous defense and how I would do things differently. He remained very calm. Throughout our conversation, he frequently quoted from the Bible; rather than referring to his incarceration as being "in prison," he called it his "bondage." That was a first. It was becoming clear that my "Come to Jesus" talk wasn't going to work. We discussed the possibility of his getting out on bail. Unfortunately, he didn't have two nickels to rub together and nobody else in his family had any money either. He told me that nobody called him Nathaniel and asked me to call him Nate.

Finally, after about 45 minutes, I decided to tell him the State's plea offer.

"Look, Nate, I believe you when you say you're innocent. And I am not telling you this in order for you to plead guilty because I will do whatever you want. But as your lawyer, I am obliged to tell you that I spoke with the prosecutor this morning, and, if you agree to plead guilty, I can get you out of jail by the end of the week."

"Well," Nate responded thoughtfully, "that's a mighty good offer if you are guilty, but I am not guilty and I am not pleading guilty."

Usually, at this point, I would have taken another shot at the plea, but not here, not with Nate. He wasn't budging. He wasn't guilty and he wasn't pleading, no way, no how. At that moment, I knew we were going to trial.

3

HUSTLING VOTES

I was born in Toronto, Canada, but I am from New Jersey, USA.

My parents moved to New Jersey when I was three, and I haven't left since. New Jersey is probably not the best state to live in; it's overcrowded and the taxes are too high. However, New Jersey is the coolest state in the Union. Of this I have no doubt. There is no debate. Think of all the famous people who hail from my state. We have Frank Sinatra and Count Basie, we have Bruce Springsteen and Jon Bon Jovi, we have Jack Nicholson and Bruce Willis, we have John Travolta and Judge Andrew Napolitano, we have Jerry Lewis and Lou Costello. As for the ladies, we have Meryl Streep, Queen Latifah, and Chelsea Handler. No other state has such a collection of talent, and I am only skimming the surface. Everyone wants to be like us, as demonstrated by the popularity of such shows as *The Sopranos, Jersey Shore,* and *Boardwalk Empire.*

Even our unofficial mascot, the Jersey Devil, is the coolest, baddest, meanest monster there is. This 13th child of the Leeds family was evil incarnate; it ate its own mother and ran through the Pine Barrens terrorizing entire towns. California is cooler? Californians take their laid-back reputation way too seriously. Legalizing weed doesn't make you cool; it means you are trying too hard. Not to mention that California has earthquakes and wildfires. New York, you say? *Fuhgeddaboudit.* New York is a big, big state—if you go 20 miles from the city you might as well be in Nebraska. Give me the Jersey edge. New Jersey's slogan shouldn't be "The Garden State"—which is admittedly ridiculous, who the hell thought *that* up?—it should be "One Hundred and Sixty-Five Miles of Cool." So, the next time you meet someone from Jersey, refrain from bringing up that stupid "Which exit?" joke and just think to yourself, "What a lucky guy."

My parents named me John, a name that belonged to my father and his father before him. My advice is not to give your children the same name as you. My mother gave me the nickname "Hanzi," which derives from the German Hans. That was all fine and good until I got old enough to have friends call me on the phone. My mother would answer, and they would ask to speak to John. Despite the fact that they were clearly kids calling, she would ask, "Do you want big John or Hanzi?" At school, everyone started calling me Hanzi as a joke, and the name stuck through high school. It was not "Jersey cool."

On second thought, do not call your son John whether or not it's a family name. While originally a fine biblical name, John has really been abused over the years. Think of it: A procurer of prostitutes is a John, an unidentified corpse is a John Doe, and a certain type of underwear is referred to as long johns. No other name has been so misused. Why not call a toilet an Adolf? Now there's a name that deserves to be shit on. But, no, a toilet is referred to as a John. My wife and I named our son Robert.

My parents made sacrifices in order to send me and my sister to nice private schools and good colleges. I went to high school with two brothers who became celebrities, of sorts: Eric and Lyle Menendez. The Menendez brothers killed both their parents in 1990, gunning them down with shotguns in their California mansion. At first, they denied any knowledge of the killing and gave the police some false leads, but when it became obvious that they did it, they claimed it was in self-defense because their father had allegedly abused them. The case went to trial, and it was pretty big news at the time. The first trial ended with a hung jury, but they were convicted in the retrial. They are now serving life sentences. When we were in school together, I spoke to Eric once or twice but didn't really know him. The only thing that I recall about him is that he admitted to liking Hall and Oates, which I found a little strange. Lyle was younger than I was, and I never interacted with him.

After high school, I attended Georgetown University in Washington, D.C. Going to Georgetown in the late 1980s was great. The drinking age in our nation's capital was 18; thus I acquired the right to drink and the right to vote on the same day. I took one of these rights very seriously, and, within a week of starting college, I had acquired the nickname "Otis," after Otis the Drunk from *The Andy Griffith Show*.

Washington, D.C. is a fantastic city, and for a freshman in college, there was so much to do and enjoy. Our dorm room housed 400 students and was modeled on a minimum security prison. Half the dorm rooms overlooked the Potomac River. Looking north, you had a clear view of the Lincoln Memorial and the city beyond. Occasionally, you could see the presidential helicopter flying along the river taking Ronald Reagan to Camp David. Unfortunately, my room was on the other side of the building overlooking a construction site. I would often be awakened at 7:00 AM by the banging of machinery, which occasionally rivaled the banging in my head.

As soon as I arrived at Georgetown, I became involved with the College Republicans and was a fairly active member. Toward the end of my freshman year, the president of the group approached me and asked if I'd like to be his successor. Being a power-hungry 18-year-old, I naturally said yes. However, we had a problem: There was a junior interested in the job. He was relatively popular and well established

within the College Republicans. And, yet, the leadership had a beef
with him for some reason, either because he was too liberal or
because he had thrown up on the vice president's couch. So they
anointed me.

I was hesitant. "But what about the election? I can't possibly
win." The president said, "Don't worry about the election, we'll just
appoint you." I protested, "Doesn't our constitution mandate elections at the end of each year?" His response was, "Hey, the Soviets
ignore their constitution whenever they want—so can we."

Still puzzled but also feeling excited, I asked, "Won't that cause
a problem?" The response was, again, "Don't worry about it." Now,
while the idea of democracy and free elections reads well on paper
and is certainly compelling in the classroom, the reality of the situation is that when you are a geeky 18-year-old freshman going up
against a junior with a fistful of votes, the sanctity of the ballot box
doesn't sound so great. I answered, "Okay, then I won't worry
about it, *Presidente*."

If you find it surprising that an 18-year-old could be so cynical,
consider this: Starting around 2002, the U.S. State Department
started pushing for free and open elections in the Middle East.
Democracy would somehow make the people want to blow us up
less, or so the theory went. The idea sounded great in think tanks
and gave the president gravitas when he spoke to the United
Nations. However, when groups such as Hezbollah started to win
elections, the idea suddenly didn't seem so bright. It seems to me I
haven't heard as much talk about "free and open" elections in the
Middle East from our government lately, and, in fact, if we were
honest about it, we'd adopt the slogan, "Democracy is great, as long
as our guy wins."

And so I entered my sophomore year as the president of the Georgetown College Republicans. I like to think I did a pretty good job. My focus was on booking speakers. I had Senators John McCain and Alan Simpson address our group. We also had Congressmen Jim Bunning (later a Senator) and Phil Crane as speakers. Phil Crane was especially interesting and went out with us for a couple of beers after his talk.

My favorite speaker, though, was the congressman from Wyoming and Republican Whip, the Honorable Richard Cheney. A lot of people see Dick Cheney as some kind of Svengali. However, my experience with him showed him to be anything but. He spoke to the College Republicans right before Christmas break in 1987. I was waiting for the congressman on Healy Circle where I was to meet him and then escort him to the lecture hall. A Mustang pulled up to the curb. The driver rolled down the window, and there he was, Dick Cheney, all by himself. He leaned over and asked, "Are you John Hartmann?" I responded in the affirmative and, like an idiot, told him he couldn't park there.

Federal law states that cars with congressional tags cannot be towed or ticketed, and the congressman just threw his Mustang into park, got out, and walked with me to the hall. We had to cut through a stinky dorm where kids were hanging out, doing whatever college kids do, like listening to loud music and drinking beer. Cheney didn't bat an eye. We arrived at the lecture hall, where I was mortified to discover that only about 10 people had showed up, possibly because it was so close to Christmas. Despite the paucity of the crowd, Cheney delivered a thoughtful and funny (yes, Dick Cheney can be *funny*) speech. Now, Cheney could have blown us off—he certainly had other, more important things to do—but he didn't. He was down to earth, gracious, and an all-around pleasant person.

I enjoyed my term as president of the Georgetown College Republicans so much that I reappointed myself to the job for my junior year. I didn't even have a board meeting; in fact, I never even convened a board meeting, believing that this could only cause problems. Thus, "the people have spoken" was supplanted by "the person has spoken," which seemed to be working just fine.

But trouble began to brew early on in my second term. A concerned student (i.e., another kid who wanted my job) complained, and I was called in to explain myself to the provost. Before the meeting, I quickly convened a board that consisted of my cronies and managed to dodge that bullet, if for no other reason than the provost was lazy, apathetic, and a Democrat. The same concerned student then lodged a complaint with the National College Republicans. I held those jokers at bay for a couple of months. Next, the school newspaper got wind of the story, and I found myself pursued by a budding Bob Woodward who saw me as a Dick Nixon in the making. I gave him an interview where I made some lame excuse and accepted full responsibility. In spite of my openness and humility, the paper ran a pretty nasty story about how the College Republicans had not held elections for a couple of years—so much for trusting the press. By the spring of 1988, the jig was up. I decided not to seek a third term as president of the Georgetown College Republicans and retired. They wouldn't have John Hartmann to kick around any longer. I had climbed to the top of the greasy pole and fallen off—but at least I had something to put on my law school application.

During my senior year, I had an easy decision to make. Attending law school just seemed like the right move, and most of my friends were doing the same. Besides, I had always wanted to become an attorney. My grades were okay, and I had really done well in my junior year and in the first term of my senior year. I took the LSATs and managed a halfway decent score. I had to decide where to apply. The University of Pennsylvania Law School was my first choice, but I knew my grades and scores weren't good enough to get me in. I had the same problem with Georgetown. A friend of mine from North Jersey suggested I look at Seton Hall University Law School. For me, attending law school in New Jersey made a lot of sense. There was no doubt that I would settle down in my beloved home state. And while "The Hall" might not be a first tier law school, it is well respected in Jersey. I ordered the application in November and filled it out. I applied in early December. According to the application package, I wouldn't know if I was accepted until March.

I went home for Christmas break and thought about other schools I might want to attend. On Christmas Eve, my father went to the mailbox and found a letter from Seton Hall University Law School inside. I was accepted. Since the letter came on the day before we celebrate our Lord's birth, I took it as a sign. I wouldn't be filling out any more applications. I was going to The Hall.

My experience at Seton Hall Law School was very different from my experience at Georgetown University. For starters, I lived at home with my parents and took the train every day from Princeton Junction to Newark. From there, it was a two-block walk to school. Today, the school is in a modern high-rise building. But when I attended law school in the early '90s, it was located in a transitional building. It was adequate but nothing to write home about. As for the neighborhood, Newark, to say the least, isn't Kansas. A classmate of mine told me that once when he was driving to school in the morning, one of his front tires blew three blocks from the campus. He pulled the car over, parked, and proceeded to change the tire. A car pulled up behind him and the driver jumped out with a tire iron and started to remove one of the back wheels from my classmate's vehicle. My friend asked him what he was doing and the bad Samaritan responded, "You got the front, I got the back."

Attending law school became more of a job than an education, and it was a job I didn't particularly like. My grades weren't that great and, in the end, I barely graduated in the top 200 of my class, being ranked number 199. With the hindsight of an attorney who has practiced law for 15 years, I can say that you learn very little that is practical in law school. And I don't mean Seton Hall Law School, I mean *any* law school. Constitutional law is such a big deal in law school, but in the real world, you rarely come across a constitutional law issue. As for property, with its "fee simples" and "running with the land," you might learn something useful if you are a historian writing a paper on "Medieval Land Reform under the Plantagenets," but it has no bearing at all on what you come across in private practice. Fee simples mean nothing when you are in the middle of a private residence closing, with impatient buyers and annoyed sellers who are nickeling and diming you over some curtains, as you nervously wait for the money wire to hit from the bank. With the possible exception of civil procedure, for which I had a really good teacher—the Dean of the School, Ronald Riccio—I didn't learn much in law school that proved useful later on.

In my second year, though, I did have one fantastic course: New Jersey Practice. It was taught by a practicing lawyer, and here, finally, was a guy who gave us useful information—like where to find free parking at the various county courthouses. When I was studying for the final exam, another student came up to me and asked what I was doing. When I told her I was preparing for the exam, she laughed and informed me that the professor gave the exact same test every year. She then gave me a copy of the exam (with the answers), which I thought was a very nice thing to do—neither one of us had a chance for law review.

Exam day came, and it was, indeed, the right test. I scored an A in that class, one of only two As I received in law school; my other A was in criminal law.

Overall, however, my law school career was disappointing. I liked the other students and made some friends, but mostly I just put my head down and tried to muddle through classes the best I could. Besides, I had discovered something much more exhilarating and fun than the law: New Jersey politics, where I had a brief and ultimately unsuccessful career as an assemblyman.

These days, if I tell someone I was an assemblyman in the early 1990s, they'll often say something like, "Wow, first politics and now criminal law—they are *so* different!" My response is that they are actually quite similar. Dealing with politicians is almost identical to dealing with criminals; the only difference between the two is that occasionally a criminal will tell you the truth. Hey, we aren't talking Wisconsin; we are talking Jersey, the most corrupt state in the nation. I once heard New Jersey referred to as the "Louisiana of the North," after a federal investigation netted about 20 political types. What an insult—to Louisiana!

The problem with corruption in New Jersey isn't that Garden Staters are more prone to commit criminal acts. They are not. The problem is we have so many levels of government. We have 566 municipalities in New Jersey (the most municipalities by far for any state) and more than 600 school districts. In addition, there are 21 counties, all with their separate governments and boards. On top of this Byzantine steaming heap of red tape and inefficiency, there is the state government and, finally, the federal government. As a result, we have all sorts of taxes including school taxes, local taxes, fire district taxes, sewage taxes (it's called an "assessment" to make the taxpayers feel less violated), county taxes, and state taxes in the form of income tax and sales tax. And, of course, there is the grand-daddy of them all, federal taxes. Government in New Jersey is one giant multi-layered money cake, oozing with taxpayer filling and covered with a rich revenue frosting. It is only natural that people want their slice, and get their slice they do. And because New Jersey has more elected and appointed positions than any other place, more people have access to the money cake, where even a few crumbs can pay off handsomely—and land you in jail for seven years if you aren't careful.

As a general rule, politicians are not to be trusted. I learned this the hard way, which should not have been necessary because when I was seven, I remember my grandfather explaining the political parties to me as follows: "There isn't a dime's worth of difference between them; they are out just for themselves." I should have listened to Grandpop. And the higher a person advances in politics, the less he can be trusted. It gets to the point that your money is safer with a crackhead than a congressman. I studied history in college, and I've always enjoyed reading, especially political biographies, and I can state that in all my studies and all my experiences, I have come across just one truly honest politician: my great-grandfather, William Eichner. He was a member of the Philadelphia Republican political machine during the 1870s and 1880s, serving as a Philadelphia councilman and later as a member of the Pennsylvania General Assembly. According to my grandmother, when he was elected to the General Assembly, he stopped going to religious services and never set foot in a church during his two terms in office, stating, "You can't serve God and politics at the same time." A truer political word was never spoken, but can you imagine a candidate saying that today?

In 1991, I decided to run for the New Jersey State Assembly in the 15th legislative district as a Republican. I ran for the same reason everyone enters politics. To change the world, you say? No. To champion a particular issue, perhaps? Nah. To send a message? Never. I ran because I needed a job. In 1991, the country was in a mild recession and summer legal jobs were hard to come by, especially for a student with average grades from a lower-tier law school. Instead, I started talking to a few people I knew and threw my hat in the ring. I was 23 years old when I declared.

The 15th legislative district as configured in 1991 was arguably the most socioeconomically diverse of the state's 40 legislative districts. Almost half of the district consisted of the City of Trenton, a Democratic bastion. Politics is a tough game, and nowhere is it played harder than in Trenton. A couple of years ago a lawyer acquaintance of mine was running the campaign for a Trenton mayoral candidate. He called me up a week before the election and asked if I could help out on Election Day. I told him I could but that I didn't know much about election law and inquired what statute books I should bring. "Books?" he said incredulously. "We don't want you to bring any legal books. We want you to bring a baseball bat."

In addition to Trenton, Princeton Borough (home of Princeton University) and Princeton Township were located in the district. Both towns are teeming with that most annoying of all creatures, the "limousine liberal." The district also comprised the blue collar towns of Ewing and Lawrence and was heavily Democratic, with registered Democrats outnumbering registered Republicans by a margin of well over three to one. Only my hometown of West Windsor, the smallest municipality by population in the district, voted reliably Republican. Indeed, the district overall was so hostile to the Grand Old Party that a Republican hadn't been elected in the 15th since "Silent Cal" Coolidge was sitting in the Oval Office. However, in 1991, things were going to be different.

New Jersey is a Democratic state. In order for the Republicans to gain any traction, the Democrats have to mess up. And in 1990, the Democrats did mess up, in a big way. In order to plug a budget gap, the newly elected Governor of the State, Jim Florio, decided to raise the income tax and the sales tax. To make matters worse, the sales tax was extended to items that had never been taxed before, such as toilet paper. It was a disaster for the Democratic Party. The voters were livid. Spontaneous rallies broke out, with irate voters throwing toilet paper at anything resembling a Democrat. In the 1990 elections, they threw the Democrats out in droves. In 1991, the voter's lust for Democratic blood had not yet been satiated, and early on, it was obvious that it was going to be a good year again for the GOP. Still, nobody—and I mean *nobody*—thought we had any chance of winning in the 15th. Surely, the Republican wave would crash on the bulkheads of Trenton and Princeton.

Being a complete political neophyte, I never "got the memo" that the 15th District was a Republican wasteland, and I just worked hard at "hustling votes," as they say in Trenton. Besides having a great Republican year to run in, I got two big breaks. First was that my surname was well known in Trenton and surrounding areas. It turned out that the Hartmann family owned a large funeral home in Trenton and had been involved in the community for years. They were no relation to me, but everywhere I went people asked me if I was related to the funeral home Hartmanns. Initially I said no, but I soon caught on and stopped denying it. (And, after all, we must have been related *somehow* back in the old country!) It helped my name recognition tremendously, being related to the owners of that funeral home. Was it underhanded of me not to issue a denial any time the question was raised? Probably, but as they say, "Losers don't legislate." Or, to paraphrase Vladimir Lenin, "Elections in New Jersey aren't girls' schools."

The second big break came in the form of my local Republican Congressman Chris Smith. This man was instrumental in helping me secure the nomination and also offered me the really sound advice to go knock on doors. As he put it, "If you walk, you win."

So I took a term off from school and spent five months, day in and day out, going door to door. Often I would go by myself, hitting door after door. If it was raining, I'd knock on doors. If it was 95 degrees with the humidity so high that you'd think you were in a tank of water, I'd knock on doors. The same thing every day. I'd knock on a door, a person would answer, and I'd say, "Hi, my name is John Hartmann and I'm running for Assembly." The next house, I'd knock and I'd say, "Hi, my name is John Hartmann and I'm running for Assembly." And so on and so on.

One day I was knocking on doors in Chambersburg, an Italian section of Trenton. I had already said "Hi, my name is John Hartmann and I'm running for Assembly" about 50 times when a door I knocked on was answered by a very attractive woman wearing nothing but a bra. I said, "Hi, my name is Assembly and I'm running for John Hartmann." I handed her my pamphlet and quickly moved on to the next door. In five months, I knocked on fifteen thousand doors, and it paid off.

In addition to raising my profile, I found that going door-to-door was a great way to get a sense of what people were thinking. And what they were thinking is that they were digging Republicans. In most of the neighborhoods where I campaigned, a Republican would expect to feel like General George Custer at the Little Big Horn, but not in 1991. I knew I was in good shape when, in one particularly tough area, a man who had probably never met a Republican, let alone voted for one, came at me with a metal pipe. He was bent on braining me until I swore I was *not a Democrat*, after which he dropped the pipe and walked away grumbling. It was unlikely he would vote for me, but at least he wasn't going to kill me. That was real progress for a Republican.

Spending what little money I had and raising a bit more, I managed to send out three mailers and purchase some lawn signs. In all, it was just enough to get my message out. My lawn signs drew attention in good part because they clearly identified my party affiliation—unheard of for a Republican running in Trenton. Almost everyone I knew thought it would backfire. But it didn't. This is not to say that what you put on your signs can't hurt you. A couple of years before my race, two local candidates with the unfortunate surnames of Cox and Ball ran for council in Ewing Township; naturally their signs read "Cox and Ball for Township Council." Ewing is home to The College of New Jersey, and more than a few students apparently thought the "Cox and Ball" signs were hilarious—no sooner was one of these signs put up than some sophomoric undergrad would snatch it for display in his dorm room. When the same team ran again a couple of years later, they'd learned a valuable lesson; with only the candidates' first names imprinted, their signs were greeted with utter and welcome apathy by the college crowd.

Campaigning was a lot of fun, and it afforded me an opportunity to speak with people whose backgrounds were very different from my own. This turned out to be very useful when I started practicing law, particularly in jury selection. But during 1991, the last thing on my mind was a law practice. I was having too good a time going to events, talking to people, eating all kinds of ethnic street food, and hitting the Irish bars.

Ignoring my great-grandfather's admonishment about mixing politics and religion, I started to attend a range of Sunday services: Catholic, Evangelical, Greek Orthodox, Hungarian Presbyterian, and Lutheran. Trenton's South Ward in particular was still full of working class folks who had their roots in Eastern Europe, and I would often be found there on Sunday mornings sharing their worship. While attending African American services, I heard about Reverend Perkins Broach, a church leader who shared some of my socially conservative positions and was described as a person I should know. I called him, and we met at a diner on South Broad Street. He was an elderly man of diminutive size, and he walked with a cane. He had a big smile. I don't know if he saw me more as a budding politician or as a project, but he seemed to take a shine to me, and he invited me to his Sunday service. I don't recall the denomination—Pentecostal or Primitive Baptist, I think—but of course I agreed.

I showed up for the 11:00 AM service a few minutes early. The church was in an old movie theater. On either side of the main entrance was an ancient ticket window. Inside, the theater had been gutted; its one large rectangular room had plain white walls that went up two stories. There was a stage with rows of seats facing it. And that was it. There was no altar. No stained glass windows. No statues. No pulpit. As a Catholic, this struck me as very spare indeed. I admit it: I like my candles. I like my incense. I like my statues of the saints. I like my chants. As I walked through the space, I could tell that this was not a candle-lighting, incense-burning crowd. On the stage, the church band was playing, and they were *rocking*. I mean *blow the roof off and praise the lord* rocking. Drums were beating, guitars were soaring, and the bass kept the undertone steady. An agitated man in a white shirt and black bowtie was more attacking the organ than playing it. If the Lord loves loud music then He was there, right there in that church. Just then Reverend Broach walked over to me and said something with his usual big smile—I couldn't hear a word he was saying over the music as I followed him to a seat at the front.

As the band continued to play, the church filled up to capacity. The music stopped, and the Reverend got up with his cane and walked to the stage. He grabbed a microphone and slowly started to preach. I can't do his sermon justice, but to put it in perspective, it lasted almost an hour but felt like 10 minutes. The sermon on this Sunday was about his conversion. Apparently, as a young man, Perkins Broach wasn't very nice. In fact, he was a hard drinking, philandering thug. He broke all Ten Commandments, some of them daily. He described his sins in detail (the statute of limitations had run out). The devil had taken him to the top of the mountain, and he liked the view. He fell deep into sin, and then from this dark abyss, from this hopelessness, the Lord slowly raised him up. The Lord took Perkins by the hand; he cut off the chains of sin. As Reverend Broach was testifying to this miraculous event, his body had changed. His voice had changed. There was no more cane. He wasn't bent over. His voice was unequivocal. He held the Bible in his right hand. "With this Bible, with this sword of the Lord I will strike down the devil!" As his sermon reached its crescendo, the band resumed playing in the background. The congregants were thanking Jesus, praising the Lord through their tears. It was Holy Bedlam. It was a sight to behold.

Then Reverend Broach said it. "Now, my brothers and sisters, I want to introduce to you a young man, a young man of promise, a young man who wants to make a difference, a young man who wants to cross the flowing River Jordan, go down to that State House, and change things! Let's give a loud *Amen* to John Hartmann. John, why don't you get up here and testify!" The people yelled "AMEN!!!"

Up until this point, I'd really been enjoying myself, but the instant the Good Reverend asked me to speak, my heart hit my stomach like a 600-pound depth charge. The game plan, I thought, was to shake a few hands over coffee and doughnuts after the service. How the hell was I going to follow Reverend Perkins Broach, that sidewinder of salvation? I took a deep breath, walked up to the stage, took the mic from the beaming Rev, cleared my throat, and … dropped a bomb. I mean a *huge* bomb. A bomb so big, a bomb so massive, that it made the bomb that hit Hiroshima look like a firecracker.

I started my testimony on that autumn Sunday morning: "I'm Catholic." With this crowd of Bible thumpers, I might as well have started off saying I was with Lucifer. I continued, "We don't have Mass like this. I am glad your Reverend got saved. Thanks for your time. It's been great." It took me less than 30 seconds to say 22 words. I handed the mic back to Reverend Broach. There was silence. I had turned a revival into a monastery. After a pause, there was a weak "Amen" from the back. I sat down and heard somebody whisper, "Something wrong with that white boy." That was it. In less time than it took to defrost a bagel in a microwave, I had probably lost 200 votes.

Despite my inability to connect with Reverend Broach's congregants that day, when election time rolled around, I felt I was in very good shape. And on Election Day, I knew I had won only half an hour after the polls closed. It was quite an experience. At 24, I was the youngest Republican ever elected to the New Jersey General Assembly, and I was still in law school. I felt as though I was really going places.

I won the election by five thousand votes, a very comfortable margin. Overall, Republicans won 58 of the 80 seats in the Assembly and gained control of the State Senate by a veto-proof margin. It was quite a night.

A couple of weeks after the vote, I went down to the State House, where the Assembly was in a lame duck session. The New Jersey State House really is a lovely building. It is the second-oldest State Capitol building in the country, after Maryland's. At the time, the Assembly and Senate chambers had just been restored. You enter the chamber through large, heavy oak doors. Before you stand 79 carved wooden desks, each with a blue leather chair. The rug is a dark blue, with a pattern of violets, goldfinches, and honey bees—the state's official flower, bird, and insect respectively. (Contrary to popular belief, the mosquito is not New Jersey's state insect, nor its bird for that matter.) In front of you is the speaker's podium, also made of wood and intricately carved, with the chiseled face of a fearsome, snickering demon—the Jersey Devil himself—on the front. The walls are painted a vibrant yellow. Abraham Lincoln once spoke in the Assembly Chamber, and it looks the part. It was beautiful then, and it remains so today.

As I was looking around, taking it all in, an elderly Democratic Assemblyman from Essex County came up to me and started to make small talk. As this engaging Italian American gentleman wrapped up the conversation, he said something that has stuck with me ever since. "Remember, Hartmann," he said, "good government is for your enemies. Pretty good government is for your friends." For me, that remark soon came to sum up how things work in Trenton.

After I was sworn into office, I was assigned to two committees: the State Government Committee, for which I served as vice chairman, and the Housing Committee. I really wanted to serve on these committees, the former because as the representative for the City of Trenton and surrounding areas, I had many state workers as constituents. As for the Housing Committee, I thought it could be useful because the lack of good and affordable housing was a problem in my district. Virtually no other assemblyman wanted to serve on these committees. I found out why later—the State Government and Housing Committees controlled no appropriations, and they couldn't regulate any businesses or professions, so lobbyists didn't care about them. And if you couldn't do anything for lobbyists, you couldn't raise any money.

We learn in elementary school civics lessons about how the government operates: The legislature has two houses. A constituent comes up with an idea and tells his elected official. In turn, the elected official writes a bill and it goes to committee. It passes through committee because it is such a great idea. The bill then goes to the other house where it goes through the same process. Then, the president, or the governor at the state level, signs the bill into law. Democracy in action. You're probably humming that *School House Rock* tune to yourself right now: "I'm just a bill, yes, I'm only a bill, and I'm sitting here on Capitol Hill."

Sorry, friends, but this is all bullshit. Here is how the legislative process *really* works. First, realize that legislators vote on thousands of bills a year. Hundreds will become law, and only a handful receive any real attention. And the legislators don't read any of them, let alone write them. They show up one day to find a stack of bills on their desk, which they promptly vote for.

Where do all the bills come from? They come from lobbyists. A business or a union or an organization pays a boatload of money to a lobbyist because they need something done. The lobbyist receives his marching orders and goes to the leadership of the party in power. In the Assembly, that's the speaker, majority leader, or a committee chairman. If the lobbyist is respected (i.e., he or she has a record of generous campaign donations), then the assemblyman asks the Office of Legislative Services to write the bill.

Once written, the bill is filed with the Assembly and given a number. It is then assigned to a committee, so the lobbyist needs to be on good terms with the chairman of the committee. The bill is given a hearing where usually nobody testifies, unless the lobbyist provides a concerned citizen or expert. After passing through committee, it is the speaker's prerogative to post the bill, which is why it's important for the lobbyist to be on good terms with the speaker and his staff. If the bill gets to the floor, it receives an up or down vote; about 99 percent of all bills that are posted will pass.

Once the bill passes the Assembly, the lobbyist goes through the same process in the Senate. If the bill passes the Senate in identical form to the bill that passed the Assembly, it goes to the governor's desk for his signature. At this point, it is again up to the lobbyist to work his magic with the Governor's Office. Lobbyists are so intertwined in the process in Trenton that when I was down there, I liked to say that I was going to hire a lobbyist myself when I needed a piece of legislation passed. I was only half joking.

Of course, this is a simplification. Sometimes issues arise that need to be addressed. During my two years in the Assembly, I was actually fairly effective in having bills enacted into law. The leadership in the

Assembly treated me pretty well, probably because they felt sorry for me. Back in college, I had written my senior history thesis on Richard Nixon's 1968 Campaign. The main focus of that campaign was "Law and Order," and I figured if it worked for Dick Nixon, it would work for me. Thus inspired by Tricky Dick, I was very aggressive in "fighting crime." Since everyone is for fighting crime, I knew it would be a good vote getter. As a result, I was responsible for a number of laws that increased sentences for certain offenses. I even sponsored the bill that created a new state penitentiary, South Woods Prison. Years later, when I visited South Woods for the first time to see a client, I sort of expected to see my picture hanging in the entrance. When I walked in, my picture wasn't there, so like a buffoon I told the guard at the metal detector, "You know, I was responsible for building this place." His response, "Good for you, it sucks." For some reason, I was made to wait an hour before I could see my client that day.

My greatest legislative achievement, the one that I am proudest of, was bringing a state-of-the-art neonatal center to a hospital in the heart of Trenton. New Jersey had been awarded federal funding for a neonatal center in an urban area. The issue was where to place it. Newark, Camden, and Jersey City all had a need for such a center. However, because those areas were represented by Democrats, and Democrats were now in the minority, they didn't have the legislative juice. I sponsored the law to bring the center to the 15th District. It may not have gotten me any votes, but I've heard stories about premature babies that were saved thanks to the special care they received at the center. To this day, I am proud that at an early age I did something that really helped ordinary people.

However, if I am remembered for anything—admittedly, a *big* if—it is for trying to raise the highway speed limit from 55 to 65 mph. I was unsuccessful, but I did lay the groundwork for the speed to be raised in the next legislative session. During my re-election bid, our unofficial campaign song was Sammy Hagar's ode to reckless driving, "I Can't Drive 55."

Being in the legislature afforded me the opportunity to meet some very interesting people. The Miss America Pageant used to be held in Atlantic City, and it was tradition that the day after Miss America was crowned she would speak at the New Jersey Assembly. I got to meet both the 1992 and 1993 winners. I also had the chance to speak at a rally with President George H. W. Bush during the 1992 presidential election. My fondest memory, though, is of the day that former football star, Congressman, and Secretary of Housing and Urban Development Jack Kemp came to town.

Thanks to the efforts of Congressman Chris Smith, Kemp visited the city of Trenton during the summer of 1992. I joined with Congressman Smith and several other local officials to meet Secretary Kemp at Miller Homes, a high-rise housing project that was run by gangs and affectionately referred to as "Killer Homes" by the locals. It was a scary place, and as we waited on the sidewalk for the secretary to arrive, with all sorts of shady characters watching us like hawks, it was unnerving. Finally, Jack Kemp pulled up to the curb.

Kemp had a reputation as one of the few Republicans who could relate to black voters, apparently because of his experience as a professional football player. From what I saw that day, the reputation was undeserved. The secretary bounded out of the car, exchanged brief pleasantries with Congressman Smith, then approached a middle-aged African American city councilman, and launched into some sort of "jivebonics" dialect.

"Yo, my man, how's it hanging?" he said to the councilman.

Clearly taken aback, the councilman responded, "Excuse me?"

Not missing a beat Kemp replied, "You know what I mean, what's up, my brotha?"

The Republican Party has sunk quite a bit since Lincoln's Emancipation Proclamation.

The secretary proceeded to walk around the entire courtyard, talking to everyone who would listen, as the congressman and councilman looked on in disbelief. I was worried about being shot, especially since I could see that the drug dealers were pissed at the interruption in their business. Only the hookers were taking it in stride, standing there smoking their cigarettes. Kemp was oblivious. Next, he entered one of the project buildings, and while I didn't want to follow, I sure wasn't about to be left alone in that concrete valley of death. The secretary went up to a man who was sitting slouched over some steps, a brown paper bag in his hand, and exhorted him to "turn it around." He spouted some crazy stuff about how he had won a football championship and was wearing a ring to prove it. The man responded to the motivational speech with a grunt, and Kemp began walking up and down the first floor hallway, making incomprehensible small talk to anyone who didn't run away fast enough. It was extremely embarrassing, yet weirdly entertaining at the same time.

In 1993, I ran for re-election. I worked just as hard as I had in my first campaign, and this time I had more money and a really fine crew anchored by Joe Glover, Bill Sabo, and Matt Sciarotta. In addition, my legislative office staff had done a very good job. I felt that I was in a strong position to win.

It didn't work out that way. The 15th district was solidly Democratic, and the pendulum came swinging back. Still, I only lost by a little over one hundred votes, probably a victim of in-fighting among local Republicans. When my term came to an end in January 1994, I held two records in New Jersey politics: I was the youngest Republican ever elected to the Assembly, and I became the youngest ex-assemblyman of either party. As it turned out, I was through with elected office for good by my mid-twenties, though as a friend of mine likes to remind me, "It is better to be a has-been than a never-was."

Postscript

If even after reading this chapter you are considering running for office, I wouldn't recommend it. The hours are long and the pay is terrible. Constituents can be testy, and you are constantly walking around with a target on your back. Furthermore, a political career is like a night of binge drinking—it rarely ends well. As a politician you will almost certainly lose, if not in your first election, then in your last.

If, knowing all this, you still intend to throw your hat in the ring, I recommend you learn from the masters and read these three books:

> *Huey Long* by Harry Williams
> *The Years of Lyndon Johnson: The Path to Power* (Vol. 1 of 4)
> by Robert A. Caro (at least read Chapter 21)
> *Nixon: The Education of a Politician, 1913–1962* by Stephen
> E. Ambrose

Then start knocking on doors.

4

WHITE SHIRT

When my foray into politics came to an end, I was ready to focus on the law. While I was running for the State Assembly, I'd taken a term off from school. Once elected, I resumed classes at Seton Hall. The school offered a day program and a night program, and traditionally students were not allowed to mix classes. But I met with the dean and they created a new program for me called "Night Time Day," in which I enrolled. The program allowed me to cram all my classes into one day a week.

The legislature met on Mondays and Thursdays. Other days, including Saturdays and Sundays, I spent as much time as possible in the office or attending events. (In fact, during my two years in the Assembly, I only took two weekends off.) I reserved Wednesdays for school; otherwise I did something political every day. As far as my education was concerned, I was like a lone gray wolf on the Arctic tundra desperately hunting for migrating caribou—I took whatever classes fit into my schedule in my search for credits. During one term, I took five two-credit classes, with a school day that ran from 8:00 AM to 10:00 PM. On these Wednesdays, my eclectic schedule included Computer Law at 8:30 AM, Law at the United Nations after lunch, a class whose name I forget at 3:00 PM, Entertainment Law at 5:05 PM (great professor), and a Law and Literature class at 7:15 PM.

I was doing the bare minimum in class. I showed up, but that was about it. I sat in the back and prayed I wouldn't be called on. I got out of my classes what I put in and received mediocre grades in all.

55

I did manage to squeeze out enough credits to graduate, though I missed the ceremony because I was out "pressing the flesh" at some senior citizen center.

My next step was to take the bar exam. Graduation was in the spring, and most grads sit for the bar exam right away in the early summer. But I was in the middle of my re-election campaign and was afraid that if I took the test and failed, the Democrats would use it as a campaign issue. I decided to wait until winter to take the exam.

I threw myself into studying for the bar. The exam consisted of two parts: a multiple choice section, and six essays covering Constitutional Law, Property, Criminal Law, Contracts, Torts, and Evidence. I spent two months studying intensively, reading all the prep books and taking practice exams. One day, I was bent over a book reading and the bridge of my glasses broke. I didn't touch them—they just fell off my face in two pieces. I looked at my broken glasses, lying on a page dealing with property law, and imagined a sword shattered on a mighty rock. Was this a sign that I was defeated? The next day when I went to get a new pair of glasses, the optometrist doing the eye exam noticed that my eyes were starting to become crossed—was I doing an unusual amount of reading? he asked.

The New Jersey bar exam lasts two days and is taken in a convention center with thousands of other prospective attorneys. The first day the multiple choice section is administered. The second day you are given six essay questions and have one hour to work on each. When I arrived at the test center, I was taken aback by the number of my former classmates who I knew had taken the test in the summer. Obviously they had failed, and it did not bode well for me.

Three months later I received my results in the mail. I had failed by a stinking one-half point! Meantime, I had just lost re-election by two-tenths of a percentage point. Somebody up there doesn't like me, I thought.

In the case of the bar, my Waterloo was Evidence, on which I bombed the essay. To this day, I have problems with evidence. During one recent trial, I kept objecting to the prosecutor's questions, and the judge asked me what specific objection I was making. I couldn't say "I don't know" in front of the jury, so I just threw out some rule. Of all the rules of evidence, the most useful I have found is the "say it real fast exception" to the hearsay rule. By the time the prosecutor objects, it is too late—the jury already heard it. This exception was not taught in law school and was not on the bar exam.

I sat for the exam again in the summer, and this time I passed comfortably. I was sworn in as a member of the bar a month later. I had my "ticket" to practice law, as they say.

What was I going to do now? Plenty of people had said they wanted to hire me when I was in the Assembly, but now that I'd lost, it seemed those job offers had dried up. I didn't feel like putting in the effort to grovel for a job with the new Republican administration. I was single and living with my parents, so with little to lose, I decided to hang out my own shingle. There is a long tradition of newly minted lawyers starting their own private practices—John Adams and Abraham Lincoln got their start that way, so why not me?

The problem with starting your own practice right out of law school is that you don't know anything. In fact, *nobody* knows less than a brand new lawyer. Back in the day, an aspiring attorney would apprentice with a practicing lawyer and learn the law by observing him in and out of court. But then the colleges and universities decided they wanted a piece of the action. They created the Law Degree, or JD, and made it a whopping three years long (or in my case four) to earn. Law schools are the big money makers for any university, a profit machine for these nonprofit organizations. The formula is simple: high fees and low expenses. They jam a bunch of students into a class and hire a few professors who rattle off grand theories and pontificate on the majesty of the law, but they fail to teach anything practical. A friend at law school observed that if law professors were required to work in the real world for one year, they would all starve to death.

Of course, law school apologists will retort that law school makes you "think like a lawyer." Well, I can get that by watching *Perry Mason* reruns or renting *To Kill a Mockingbird*, in which Gregory Peck will not only show you how to think like a lawyer, he'll show you how to *dress* like a lawyer, which is much more important than thinking like one. Nothing—and I mean nothing—demonstrates that you are going to kick some legal butt more than wearing a seersucker suit on a hot, humid July day. There you are sitting at counsel table, cool on the inside and cool on the out because of your threads, going up against opposing counsel, who is sweating like a pig in his gray wool pinstripe. You have already won. I don't care if your opponent was the editor of the *Yale Law Review* and you got your degree from a box of Cocoa Puffs, you've won before you even open your mouth.

Anyhow, once you've graduated, passed the bar, and mortgaged your future with student loans, then the really important stuff—like how to actually file a bail motion or get street clothes to a client who is incarcerated or even where to stand when you are addressing the court—you learn *after* law school. In other words, you have to start your apprenticeship.

With my apprenticeship, politics opened a door for me. In my travels, I had met a freeholder from the neighboring county of Middlesex named Roger Daley. Roger's political story was similar to mine; he ran for freeholder in 1990 and won by a large margin, benefitting from the backlash against Governor Jim Florio and his tax increases. Even more impressive, he won a close re-election in 1993. When Roger and I met, we hit it off, and he suggested that I come work for him or at least work out of his law office. The office was right across from the Middlesex County Courthouse in New Brunswick.

I thought Roger was a great guy, and, with no other prospects, I figured, why not? I didn't do much legal work initially, as I was busy plotting my return to the Assembly. When it eventually became clear there would be no rematch, I resigned myself to the fact that I would have to actually work for a living.

Roger was a real character. He had grown up in central New Jersey and had attended Rutgers University. He fought in Vietnam where he was an MP. He came home, got married, and, disillusioned with the war, fell into a Bohemian lifestyle. Eventually, he became motivated to attend law school, graduating at the age of 38 and starting his own law practice shortly thereafter. In the meantime, he underwent a religious conversion; he remains a very devout Catholic to this day.

I didn't make any money during my years with Roger—I don't think Roger made much, either—but it was a great time in my life. The man was incredibly funny, for one thing, and we spent hours in his office just shooting the breeze. His desk was a big conference table over which he spread all sorts of papers and files and religious cards. He loved his religious cards, and, like a salesman of salvation, he seemed to be hawking a new saint or prayer every week.

"You have to say a novena to Blessed So-And-So, she is *powerful*,"
he'd insist. He told me all sorts of wild tales about politics, practicing law, and Vietnam. A crew of lawyers would often come by to
swap stories, and, as it turned out, it was very good to be Roger's
friend. Most of the lawyers who stopped by on a regular basis ended
up on the bench.

Roger also gave me sound advice. One day he said, "John, if you
want to be a criminal defense attorney, there are three things you
should know."

I give you now the "Three Legal Tenets of Roger Daley":

1. Whenever you meet a criminal client for the first time, ask
    "What's your jacket like?"

2. Always read the statute.

3. Whenever you have good news for a client, ask for money.

Rules 2 and 3 are self-explanatory. As for Rule 1, "jacket" is
slang for a person's criminal record, otherwise known as a criminal
case history (CCH). Asking a defendant about his jacket immediately gives your client the impression that you are "down with the
lingo" and probably know what you are talking about—in other
words, it's a quick way to establish street cred. You can also gain
valuable information about your client with this question. If you ask
about his jacket and he looks at you like you're from Mars and says,
"I didn't wear one today," then this is probably the first time he's
been arrested. If he says, "I won't lie to you, my jacket isn't that
great," then you probably have a client with about 10 arrests and
two upper court convictions. And if he responds by saying, "I don't
have any bodies on my jacket," then it's likely a tree had to be cut
down to produce enough paper to print his CCH.

Looking back today, with more than 15 years of law practice behind me, I can say with confidence that the "Three Legal Tenets of Roger Daley" are excellent rules to follow. They have always served me well.

There is, by the way, one useful corollary to Roger's rules. If you achieve a good result for a client, never admonish him with the words, "Don't get in trouble again." He probably *will* get into trouble again and may be too embarrassed to call you. The right approach, when you are parting ways with a happy client, is to say, "If you ever get in trouble again, give me a call."

One day, sitting in the office, Roger said to me, "You know John, I think you should do pool work—that's how I got started. Do you want some?"

As I explained earlier, pool cases are cases where the public defender's office represents more than one co-defendant. Because a law firm cannot usually represent co-defendants, the public defender's office will keep one and "pool" out the others. The way it works is that an attorney on the pool list is called up by a secretary in the public defender's office. He or she has a day or two to pick up the file. Pool work paid little more than peanuts back in the mid-90s—$15 an hour for work out of court and $22.50 for work while you were "on your feet" in court. I didn't have anything else to do when Roger asked me, so I responded in the affirmative.

Roger knew a bunch of people at the Middlesex County public defender's office, and they agreed to give me some cases as long as he oversaw my work. A few days later, I got a call from the public defender's office. They needed a pool attorney in court right away— that morning, in fact. I could go right over to court, have my client arraigned on a drug case, and enter my appearance before the judge. The file would be ready for pickup in the afternoon. When I heard

this news, I responded, "Okay, I'll be right over." I put on my jacket
and walked out the door of Roger's office into what would turn out
to be a whole new world.

I crossed the street and went into the courthouse, passed through
a metal detector, and made my way to the elevator for the fifth (and
top) floor, the floor where the criminal law judges sat. I exited the
elevator and walked to my left. On one side of the hall were rows
of seats; on the other were the doors to the courtrooms. I walked
briskly down the hall and approached a public defender I knew. She
told me the judge was on break and I had a few minutes to talk with
my client. She introduced us, said "good luck," and walked away.

The client was a 42-year-old African American man. From his
appearance, it seemed that life hadn't been kind to him. He was
unshaven and poorly dressed. He spoke English but with an accent
so thick I could barely understand him. He also had one of the lazi-
est eyes I've ever seen. As I talked to him, his left eye looked
directly at me while his right eye pointed sharply up and to the
right. He smelled as though he had finished a Wild Irish Rose binge
about five hours earlier. Between the slurred speech, the lazy eye,
and the fact that I knew nothing about criminal law, I got a bit dis-
oriented trying to follow his story. But this is the gist of it.

My client was in a second-floor back room of some flophouse in
downtown New Brunswick, where, he said, he was going to "get it
on" with one of his ladies. He pointed out the object of his affec-
tion, who was also one of his co-defendants, seated on a chair about
10 feet away. The woman smiled nicely at me and waved. She
looked to be in her mid-sixties. He continued his story. He was on
the bed. His pants were down, and he was about to satisfy his sweet
tooth with some "granny candy." All of a sudden a young man burst
through the door and threw down 10 loose bags of heroin, each

stamped with the numbers "911." Two seconds later, three hard charging cops entered behind the interloper of love. Taking note of the bags of heroin, the cops put everyone in cuffs, including Romeo.

As my client is telling me this story, I am focusing on his left eye, taking his words in, growing more and more excited, thinking to myself, "This is great, this is fantastic, you can't make stuff like this up." A little light bulb went off in my head and I thought, "I want in!" I was Saul on the road to Damascus, and this face before me, with the three-day stubble and blankly staring bloodshot right eye, was the face of my future. It was like the day when, at 15, I heard the first four songs on *Van Halen I*, or the time when, over the summer between high school and college, I read *Modern Times* by Paul Johnson. It was like seeing my future wife for the first time in that pretty pink sweater. It was a life-changing moment.

By this time, the judge was about ready to go back on the bench and everyone was heading back into the courtroom. I was an attorney so I headed up to a reserved area in the front. I sat down and said to the attorney sitting next to me, "I must be in the front row," doing my best Bob Uecker imitation. The other attorney acknowledged my stupidity with a grunt. "Act like you've been here before," he must have thought. There were only a few cases left for the morning session and, in short order, the judge called my case. I walked to the defense counsel table. Next to the defense counsel was the prosecutor's counsel table, which was, as always, closest to the jury box. My client stood next to me. It was time for the arraignment. Roger had told me what to say, and I had written it down on a legal pad. For the first time in my life I said:

"Good morning, Your Honor. John Hartmann on behalf of the defendant."

I continued. "At this time we waive the reading of the indictment and enter a plea of not guilty. I acknowledge receipt of discovery and ask for a continuation of bail."

I was on my way.

The case turned out well for my client. The prosecutor ended up dismissing it. The co-defendant who had so rudely interrupted my client's intimate moment went to trial on another matter and was convicted. He pled guilty to the possession of the 10 bags of heroin, thereby exonerating my client and his girlfriend, for a deal that ran the sentence concurrent to the charge where the jury found him guilty. In other words, to use prevailing jargon, he cut my client loose and took the weight.

The public defender's office began to assign me cases on a regular basis. I would receive a phone call from a secretary asking me to pick up a file and then walk five blocks to the nondescript building at the end of a dead end street next to raised train tracks that housed the public defender's office. Across the street from the office was a group home for the mentally ill, and often as I arrived, the residents could be found walking aimlessly up and down the street in a drug-induced fog. The distinctive way they meandered was referred to as the "Thorazine Shuffle." When they were out in force, I felt like I was in a scene from *Night of the Living Dead*.

The Middlesex County public defender's office was staffed by an excellent group of lawyers. One of the attorneys, James Pfeiffer, took me under his wing. Jim was about 50 and had earned the nickname "Dr. Pfeiffer." The first time I had any interaction with Jim I was sitting in a side office in the courthouse talking to a few other lawyers. In sauntered Jim, like the burned-out office manager checking on a couple of goof-off employees. He looked around and said in a contrived, insincere voice, "Guys, you are doing a hell of a job. Keep up the good work." Not waiting for a response, he simply turned around and walked out. I thought the encounter was puzzling and after a moment I asked, "Who was that?" Somebody said, "That's Jimmy Pfeiffer. He's a little crazy."

Jim was apparently a very effective trial lawyer in his day, but his real skill was working out cases. He had a God-given knack for getting probationary offers for clients with fairly serious criminal records. Often, on the basis of his jacket, a client would be facing time, but Jimmy would somehow manage to keep him out of jail. He was an expert at schmoozing prosecutors, especially the female prosecutors. They would offer his client five years in state prison, and Jimmy would start working them, using the Pfeiffer magic. "But, Jim, your client was caught with 50 bags of crack and he has a CCH as long as my arm," the prosecutor might say. Jimmy would respond, "Hey, that doesn't make him a bad person." He'd make up some story about the defendant's mother or his kid and how the defendant had seen the light. After Jimmy spent about 10 minutes making arguments, appealing to the prosecutor's sympathy, and flat out begging, the prosecutor would offer probation on the condition that the client took the offer that day. If another prosecutor was listening, he'd often roll his eyes, laugh, and say, "There goes Dr. Pfeiffer!" Many prosecutors had been on the receiving end, and all of them knew Jim's shtick.

I learned two things from Jim Pfeiffer. First, the reason he was so good at what he did was that he had empathy for his clients. He really felt for them. The lesson here is that if you want to be able to sell something to the prosecutor, you have to believe deep down that your client deserves one more chance. Most people think drug dealers, robbers, and criminals in general are scum. Not Jim. In his universe, people might do bad things but rarely were they intrinsically evil. In my experience, I have found this to be true. I have only ever represented four people who I believed to be sociopathic. One of these "Four Horsemen of Pathology" was actually quite pleasant— it's just that he'd have no compunction about beating you over the head with a crowbar for five dollars.

The other thing I learned from Dr. Pfeiffer is the importance of begging. When all else fails, beg. In criminal law, most of your clients are guilty of *something*, so you'd better get good at begging, and get good at it fast. I learned from watching the king. After a tough round of negotiations, I often think to myself, "Four years of law school, and all I do is beg."

I went to Jim whenever I needed advice on a case. He would usually invite me up to his house in East Brunswick on a Saturday, and we'd sit and review my file. For my first trial, I went up there two or three times to prepare. He gave me lots of good advice, but he also played a trick on me. When I asked what I should say during my opening to the jury, Jim told me, "Start off by saying your client is facing a lot of jail time if convicted." Any practicing lawyer knows that it is impermissible to mention what penalties your client is facing. I didn't know this small fact, so during my first trial, the prosecutor gave his opening and I followed by stating right off the bat, "Ladies and gentlemen of the jury, if my client is convicted, he is facing a lot of jail time."

"Objection! I want a mistrial!" yelled the prosecutor as he jumped to his feet. The judge called us to side bar, looking really pissed. We had just spent all morning picking a jury; the last thing he wanted was to declare a mistrial and spend the afternoon picking another.

"Mr. Hartmann, what are you doing?" he sternly asked through his teeth, his face red. I did what anyone would do in that situation: I threw Jimmy under the bus.

"Ah, Your Honor, James Pfeiffer told me to say it." The judge looked at me, shook his head, and started to chuckle. The prosecutor, who had been putting people in jail since the year I was born, burst out laughing. "Sounds like something Jim would do," the judge commented. Nothing further was said and I went back to my opening.

A week later, I ran into Jim and started haranguing him over the dirty trick. "Wait a second, John, what happened in your case?" he asked.

I said, "The jury hung and the prosecutor gave us a plea agreement for no jail."

"And this was the case where your defendant had a pound of cocaine and a Luger pistol in the trunk of the car he was driving, right?"

"Yes," I responded.

"And he admitted to knowing about the drugs to the cops?" asked Jim. Again I responded in the affirmative. "This guy was as guilty as sin, wasn't he?"

"Why, yes he was," I said.

"He was facing 15 years in jail and you got him probation," Jim said.

"Right again, Jim," I answered, starting to see his point.

"John," Jim said, "always listen to your Uncle Jimmy."

Doing pool work was a great way to learn how the system worked. Criminal law is fairly complicated and takes some getting used to. You have to learn the penalties that a defendant is facing. For instance, in New Jersey, there are four degrees of crimes. First and second degree crimes are the most serious, including murder, sexual assault, and armed robbery. Most first degree offenses carry 10–20 years in state prison, with some exceptions such as murder, where a defendant can be sentenced up to life, and aggravated manslaughter and carjacking, where a defendant can receive up to 30 years. Second degree offenses, which are also considered very serious, carry a penalty of five to 10 years. A defendant faces three to five years incarceration for third degree offenses and up to 18 months in state prison for fourth degree offenses. If you are convicted of a first or second degree offense, it is almost certain that you will go to state prison. However, for most third and fourth degree offenses, if you have no criminal record, there is something called "presumption of non-incarceration"; it is presumed you will not go to state prison, though you may get up to a year of county time.

Once a person pleads guilty or is found guilty at trial, how much jail time they receive is determined by weighing what are called statutory aggravating and statutory mitigating factors. On top of that, you have to worry about periods of parole ineligibility for drug offenses and for violent offenses. For instance, a defendant who is caught dealing drugs within one thousand feet of a school, even if it is midnight during August, faces a period of parole ineligibility. Usually if a defendant is sentenced to, say, four years incarceration, he can go before the parole board in 10 months. However, if he receives a stipulation of parole ineligibility of two years (the slang would be "four with a two year stip"), he has to stay two years in state prison before he can see the parole board. The stip is called the "back number," and the actual sentence is called the "front number." And I haven't even talked about discretionary and mandatory extended terms and parole "hits."

If this sounds confusing, it is. And it simply cannot be learned just by reading the Criminal Statute Book (referred to as the "2C," which is its title under New Jersey law). You can memorize the 2C backward and forward, and you still won't know how it really works. You have to experience it to figure it out, and you can't fake it. You can't fake it because if you don't know the law, you can really hurt your client. In civil law, if you make a mistake, you are only costing your client money, and he can sue you for malpractice. If you mess up in criminal law, your client will be going to jail for an extra two years, and he can never get that time back.

You can't fake it with your clients. If defendants know one thing, it is stips and hits and back numbers and "numbers running wild." Your guy may have failed out of tenth grade and have been addicted to crack for 15 years, but he knows how much time he is facing, down to the day when he sees parole for his third bid. You have to be able to talk to your client on his level: "Your offer is five with a 24-month stip. If you want to work it out, I can file a few motions and maybe get your front number to a four and your back number to 15 months." If you can't talk like this, your client will lose all confidence in you and you will lose control. If you lose control, you might as well sign a trial memo at the arraignment date.

I threw myself into criminal law. Middlesex County has a number of very good criminal defense attorneys, and I picked up a lot by going to court and just watching them work. One attorney in particular was worth observing: Kenneth Weiner. Weiner doesn't practice law anymore, but back when I started, he was the heavy hitter in Middlesex. Every chance I had I went to see him, whether it was the opening of a murder trial or a bail motion. He was smart. He was entertaining. He was successful. One day, I was talking to Jim about emulating Ken Weiner. In response, Jim said, "John, you can't be like Kenny Weiner. You are too different from him. My advice is to be yourself. If you try to be somebody else, a jury will see right

through you. Be yourself." Again, it was great advice from Dr.
Pfeiffer.

I took every case I could lay my hands on and asked all sorts of
lawyers for their advice. I also hit the books in my own fashion,
studying the law and writing briefs. And I started to dress like a
criminal attorney—or at least like I *thought* a criminal attorney
should dress. Gone were the white and navy-blue button-down
shirts from Republican politics. In were red, black, and French-blue
shirts (the latter enjoyed a renaissance in the mid-90s). Out were the
Brooks Brothers striped ties; my favorite tie was one I bought at the
Philadelphia Museum of Art. Against a black field was a design of
about 20 snarling red pit bull dogs, each with a broken chain around
its neck. It was awesome, especially worn over a black shirt.

I grew a goatee, and I guess because I'm bald on top with dark
hair, people started calling me "Lenin." I thought that was great.
"Yeah, baby—Revolution!" Walking into court with my file, my pit
bull tie, and my Lenin look, I thought I was really *bad*. In actuality,
I probably looked like a dope—about as cool as an eight-track tape.
Nowadays, the goatee is gone, I haven't worn the French-blue shirt
in a decade, and my closet is home to a large collection of striped
ties. I can no longer rely on the good graces of the public defender's
office for work; I need people to actually hire me, so I can't afford
to look like a fool. But I sure had a lot of fun in my clown suit back
in the day.

As I grew into my role, I also started to curse—a *lot*. Early on,
Roger told me that trial attorneys always cursed, so when I talked
to other lawyers and clients (at least my male clients), I started to
drop the "F bomb," usually in every sentence, sometimes twice in a
sentence, and once or twice I even managed three times in a sentence. I remember one day in Camden hanging out with two bail

bondsmen in their office. I have no recollection of why the hell I was in Camden, but I was sitting there cursing away, talking shit. One of the bail bondsmen, a big Hispanic dude with a million tattoos, looked at me and said, "Man, you curse too much." I thought to myself, "Yes! I have arrived."

Living the criminal defense lifestyle presented its risks. While I might have been able to put on a good show, career criminals could see right through me. When I was just starting out, I was assigned to represent a defendant on a third degree drug charge. He had an extensive criminal history with about six upper court convictions and was currently in jail with no hope of bailing out. If you are incarcerated in Middlesex, the Sheriff's Department transports you over to the courthouse where you sit in a bullpen in the basement until you are brought up to court. There's a section in the basement set aside for attorney–client conferences, which is where I met my new client for the first time. He immediately sized me up as a "greenhorn"—no way was he going to trial with me. He made it clear that he intended to plead guilty and wanted me to get the best deal possible.

As I was leaving he asked, "Hey, Mr. Hartmann, can you get me a pack of cigarettes?" Wanting to get off on the right foot with him, I agreed. I bought a pack after lunch and brought it down to him before we went to court. We were sitting down when I took the pack out of my pocket and started to hand it to him. "Whoa," he said, "not so obvious." He took a piece of paper, covered up the pack and slipped it into his pocket in one quick movement. Later on I told another attorney about my nice new client and what I'd done for him.

"No wonder your client likes you," he said. "That pack of cigarettes is worth like one hundred dollars in jail." He added, "It was a stupid move on your part—that was contraband, and you could have been charged." It wasn't the only time that my inexperience made me lose sight of the fact that I was, after all, dealing with criminals. I did eventually smarten up.

Criminal law opened up a whole new world to me, one I didn't even know existed. I'd grown up in the suburbs and attended private school and then college, and though I had spent time in Trenton while serving in the State Assembly, the people I was reaching out to were mostly hard-working, church-going folks. It wasn't until I became a public defender that I discovered this parallel society running along New Jersey's underbelly; a society built around drugs, addiction, crime, and punishment, with its own language, rules, and mores.

I was exposed to an example of the rules of this parallel society in my second trial, where I was representing an illegal alien. He had been picked up by the Perth Amboy Police on a domestic violence charge and had apparently resisted arrest. When he was brought back to the police station, he started to get a beating from the police, under the orders of the lieutenant in charge of the shift. In spite of being handcuffed, he somehow managed to escape. He ran a couple of blocks, his hands cuffed behind his back, no shoes on his feet, with blood running down his face. The police re-apprehended him and brought him back to the station where, again under the orders of the lieutenant, he was given another beat down. (One of the rules of the street is that if you make the police run, you are going to get a beating.)

My client was indicted for resisting arrest and escape. We went to trial and beat the escape charge but went down on resisting arrest. The judge ended up giving him a flat four; this was the original offer so we didn't give up anything by "taking it to the hoop." But when the verdict came in, I was taken aback. I had worked so hard on the case that I expected to win. In other words, I had believed my own bullshit, which is actually quite typical in trials. Initially, the jury said "not guilty," and I was ecstatic, but this was quickly followed by the guilty verdict. I put my head down and must have looked upset. I felt somebody patting me on the back saying, "It's okay." I looked around to find that it was my client, comforting *me*!

One thing that struck me about this client was how he referred to the lieutenant. He didn't call him the lieutenant. He didn't call him the chief. He didn't call him the head police officer. He referred to him as "The White Shirt." "The White Shirt ordered the beating" and "The White Shirt stood there with arms crossed." The reason why the lieutenant was referred to as "The White Shirt" was, not surprisingly, because he wore a white shirt while the other officers wore blue. However, coming from the mouth of my client in a thick South American accent, it made the lieutenant seem like a malevolent character, as if from a James Fenimore Cooper novel, lording over a primordial land.

As a picture of this parallel society began to emerge for me, one lesson I quickly learned from my clients was that when it came to this world, *they* were the experts who knew the score. I was a know-nothing, a nobody. This fact was brought home for me in another early case, in which I represented a defendant whose street name was "Earthquake." Earthquake had been the subject of an investigation, and the police had applied to a judge for a warrant to search his home. Because he was known as "Earthquake," the police assumed my client was dangerous and asked for a no-knock warrant, meaning they could break his door down without any warning. When they busted into Earthquake's apartment without knocking, they found a significant stash of drugs.

Earthquake wanted me to challenge the validity of the search warrant because the police had not knocked. I told him that he had no case because the police had a no-knock warrant. He insisted I file the motion. I finally relented, knowing it would be a waste of time. The motion was heard and, as I expected, we lost. Because we had heard the motion, my client's offer went up from five years with an 18-month stip to seven with a three-year stip. He took the deal and went to state prison.

The story does not end there. Two years later, I was walking around the courthouse and saw somebody who looked vaguely familiar. After walking by him, I suddenly realized it was Earthquake, and I was surprised since his stip was not yet up. I asked around and got the story. From prison, Earthquake filed an appeal on the no-knock issue. The appellate division shot him down. He then appealed to the New Jersey Supreme Court. The Court agreed to hear the case and, lo and behold, the seven justices agreed with Earthquake. The Court found that the police must have a reasonable suspicion and articulable reason as to why they need a no-knock warrant, and ruled that an ominous-sounding nickname is insufficient to merit the no-knock rule. His conviction was over-turned. Earthquake was right, after all, and there is a published New Jersey State Supreme Court case that proves it.

After learning of Earthquake's victory, I began to take my clients' suggestions more seriously. Absent subpoenaing the President of the United States, if a client tells me to investigate something or raise a certain issue, I do it. After all, it worked for Earthquake, so it just might work for them.

5

BABALORISHA

I did pool work for the Middlesex public defender's office for about two years, during which time a new head public defender took over. Tom Sullivan had worked his way up the ladder in the Monmouth County public defender's office and was transferred to Middlesex to run the show. While in Monmouth, Tom had gained a reputation as a top-notch trial attorney and had been involved in some high-profile capital cases. It was well known at the time that Tom was looking to become a judge in Monmouth County. In order to be nominated to the bench in New Jersey, you basically need support from two sources: your local political organization and your local state senator. Tom was a Democrat and had the support of his local Democratic organization. But his state senator was a Republican whom he didn't know. Jim Pfeiffer—ever the king of inter-office politics—told him that I could be useful in the Republican department. Tom called me in for a meeting.

"So John, Jim Pfeiffer tells me you were in the State Assembly."

"Yes, I was."

"A Republican?"

"Of course. Ronald Reagan is my main man."

"Do you know Senator Joe Perilli?"

"Yes, I do."

"And do you feel comfortable enough to call him?"

"Sure do. I've got his home number. I'll call him tonight."

"John, I think you and I are going to get along just fine."

Just to be clear, Tom Sullivan was a very good lawyer and deserved to be a judge. I didn't mind helping him one bit. From the time we met, it took about three years for him to get his robe, and it wasn't just handed to him. As of the writing of this book, he is the Presiding Criminal Judge in Monmouth County. I get to Monmouth County a couple of times a year and try to stop by to say hi. He always has time to talk to me, and I have never heard anyone say anything bad about him, which is pretty rare for a judge.

Now, at this time all I wanted to do was to try cases. I didn't care what the case was, who the defendant was, or what the facts were—if it meant going before a jury, I wanted a piece of it. In my pursuit of trials, the friendship I developed with Tom Sullivan paid off; he started to assign me cases that were trial bound.

The first case he gave me involved a client named Kyree Jones. Kyree was notorious in Middlesex County. He had been through the system for years, and nobody ever wanted to represent him because he was a mean, nasty bastard. This time around, he had picked up a drug distribution charge and been assigned a female public defender. Kyree made her life so miserable that she went crying to Tom Sullivan, who promptly relieved her of the case and dumped it on me.

I went to see Kyree at the county jail, waiting for him in a small office off the common area. In he walked, a six foot three, power-fully built African American. Usually when I meet a client for the first time, he will respectfully call me Mr. Hartmann; on occasion he might refer to me as John. I'm rarely called anything else. In Kyree Jones's case, my name was "motherfucker" right from the start. The first words out of his mouth were, "Who the fuck are you, motherfucker?" I introduced myself as his lawyer and he immediately said to me, "We ain't got nothing to say, motherfucker. We are taking it to trial, motherfucker. I don't want to fucking even see you until we are putting 12 people in the box, motherfucker." At this point, I began to correct him, pointing out that you actually pick 14 jurors—12 deliberating and two alternatives—but he had already left the room.

It was the same every time we met. Kyree would say to me, "I was framed by the cops, motherfucker. Why are we here, motherfucker? I want a trial now, motherfucker."

Finally, after months of this abuse, we had our trial date. Kyree was sitting next to me at counsel table. He had on an ill-fitting polyester suit that I had gotten from the public defender's office. You can't be tried in prison clothes (an appellate case decided that) so it was up to me to get him something appropriate to wear for trial. The public defender's office had accumulated a strange assortment of dress clothes for defendants—a wardrobe the attorneys referred to as the "PD Boutique." I had selected an outfit from the PD Boutique that morning and taken it over to the holding cell before court. While the suit was cheap, I admired the tie, which was yellow with smiley faces on it—I felt it suited my client perfectly. As I handed Kyree his trial clothes, I briefly spoke to him, commenting on the fact that he was finally going to get his trial.

"About time, motherfucker," he said.

There's typically about a half-hour wait for potential jurors to enter the courtroom and that time is often spent talking with your client. Usually, it's a good conversation; you have prepared for the trial and are ready. Your client is ready. You have spent time together and established a rapport, and you'll often make small talk about family, sports, or what's on television. This is the calm before the storm, most of the time. On this morning, however, I was not sharing any warm and fuzzy banter with Kyree Jones. He didn't like me and I didn't like him. We both sat there, motionless, seething on the inside. The smiley-face tie I had so carefully selected had not made Kyree any friendlier. All of a sudden, the jury pool entered. Some 60 people walked into the courtroom and took their seats.

After the last prospective juror entered the courtroom, I felt a tug at my elbow. It was Kyree. He leaned over and said to me, "Excuse me, Mr. Hartmann"—all of a sudden I was Mr. Hartmann—"everyone is *white.*"

I had also noted the paleness of the jury pool when everyone walked in, but I turned around and looked to make certain. Sure enough, there was not an African American in the bunch.

I leaned over and said in a soft voice, "Yes, Kyree, everyone is white."

After a brief pause, he responded, "Mr. Hartmann, is that usual?"

"Well, you know, Kyree," I said, "when they say that you are to be tried by a jury of your peers, they don't really mean it."

"Ah, I see. Um, Mr. Hartmann, what was the prosecutor's offer?"

"The offer was five with a two," I said.

"Mr. Hartmann, do you think you can get that for me?"

I responded, "I will see what I can do."

The case of *State of New Jersey v. Kyree Jones* was over within one hour. Good riddance!

A short time after this case resolved, Tom called to say he wanted to sit down with me. I went to his office that afternoon. People were happy with the job I was doing and he wanted to give me a promotion. Tom offered to make me a "per diem" attorney as opposed to being a pool attorney. As I sat there listening to him, I felt like a minor league ballplayer whose coach was telling him he was being sent up to the big leagues. I thought about the offer for one minute and accepted. It was a wise decision.

A per diem attorney is, for all intents and purposes, a full-time public defender who can maintain his private practice. The benefits are substantial. Instead of being paid a low hourly rate per case and having to wait until two months after the matter was resolved to be compensated, I would be paid a flat rate of $180 dollars per day (the rate went up shortly thereafter to $225 per day). In addition, I could keep my private practice and do other work on the side. Because I would usually only be required to be in court on Mondays for status conferences and Fridays for sentencings and motions, I would have a lot of time to build up private cases. What's in it for the State? Mainly, since a per diem attorney is not a state employee, the State saves money not having to pay for benefits, such as medical insurance, sick leave, and pension. The State of New Jersey and I thus entered into a beautiful, symbiotic relationship.

Right out of the box, I was placed on a trial team and assigned to represent indigent clients before the Honorable Carol Markashevsky, a former prosecutor who had been on the bench for 15 years. As a judge, Markashevsky had the reputation of being prosecutor-oriented. I found this to be partially true. It was reported that she had *never* granted a motion to suppress evidence, and this was true of the trials I was involved in. In fact, she almost always ruled with the prosecutor on issues both before and during trial. As an example of her purported pro-State bias, I was involved in a trial where the defendant attempted to burn down his girlfriend's house after she broke up with him. The girlfriend and her parents were in the house when he tried to set it on fire. We were in the process of selecting a jury. The judge was asking prospective jurors if they or a close member of their family had been the victim of a crime. The potential juror in seat seven, a pleasant looking elderly woman, raised her hand and asked for a side bar.

We all came to side bar and what she told us was the equivalent of having cold water thrown in our faces. She said her daughter had been murdered by her boyfriend. Upon hearing this startling story, the judge said, "My dear, I am so sorry. Do you still think you can be a fair juror?" After a moment's hesitation, the woman responded that she thought she could. The judge said, "Well, then I will keep you on." I was thinking to myself, what the hell? If there was ever a juror who was prejudiced against a particular type of defendant (justifiably so, I might add), this was it. I decided then and there to knock juror seven off the jury at my first chance. But then the lady said, "Judge, there is one more thing. I am looking at the defendant, and I feel sorry for him." Judge Markashevsky responded, "In that case, I am going to use my discretion to exclude you from the jury."

While Judge Markashevsky was rough on defendants up through trial, once the case was over and the defendant was convicted, she was actually quite fair and had the reputation of imposing relatively lenient sentences. Also, she was very reasonable in terms of working with attorneys. If you couldn't be in court on a certain day or if you needed to be somewhere else at a certain time, she always did her best to accommodate your schedule. In her own fashion, Judge Markashevsky also gave advice ("Mr. Hartmann, sometimes the things you do make no sense."), and she even intervened with the prosecutor once after I made a really big mistake. All in all, a defense attorney could do worse than to appear before Carol Markashevsky.

My public defender partner who also appeared before Judge Markashevsky was Richard Barker. Everyone called Richard "Red" because of his Van Gogh–like red beard. He was a true believer: For Red, defending the downtrodden and marginalized wasn't a job, it was a cause. He was older than I was, sported a pony tail, and was quite a character. He had many interesting stories to tell; my favorite concerned his Woodstock experience. On the last day of the festival, a Monday morning, Red was sleeping in the mud when he was awakened by the sound of a guitar that was unlike anything he'd ever heard. He raised himself from the muck and ran over to the stage to find Jimi Hendrix playing for the early risers. Red told this story in highly entertaining fashion.

Red and I complemented each other well. He was generous in giving me advice, and I believe he looked after me at first, probably because Tom had asked him to. In time, we became a pretty good team. At one point, a new prosecutor was assigned to our judge—a guy who obviously wanted to give the impression of being really tough. All his plea offers involved jail time. Even for cases where under the law the defendant should not go to jail, his offer inevitably involved a period of incarceration. I talked to Red about this situation one morning in court and he told me to meet him in his office during lunch. Lunchtime came and there I was, sitting in Red's messy office, a big poster on the door of Kid Rock flipping the bird while drinking white lightning out of a jar. "Red, what are we going to do about this new prosecutor?" I asked. Red's response was straightforward, "Fuck him. I am not pleading anyone out." My response was, "Yeah, fuck him. I am not pleading anyone out either." The meeting was over.

For one month, Red and I didn't plead any of our clients guilty. If this doesn't sound like a big deal, it was. Public defenders represent approximately 50 percent of the cases before a judge, and on average, we would each have approximately 10–15 guilty pleas a month. With our silent strike, Red and I had jammed a crowbar in the spokes of the wheel of justice.

Judges in New Jersey must regularly report the number of cases they've resolved to the Administrative Office of the Courts (AOC), and if they don't move enough cases, it creates problems for them. What specific problems I haven't quite figured out, but the AOC can strike terror in the heart of even the toughest judge. (I've heard judges talk about the AOC the way characters in a Solzhenitsyn novel might talk about the KGB.) After a couple of weeks of our plea strike, Judge Markashevsky's numbers started looking really bad and I'm sure the AOC was on her mind. She called the prosecutor, Red, and me in for a meeting. While we liked Her Honor, Red and I really didn't care about her numbers; we just wanted to keep our clients from getting screwed. The prosecutor apparently didn't care about the judge's problem either, because Mr. Tough Guy was laying down the law and sticking to his guns.

But Judge Markashevsky wasn't about to let some punk prosecutor bring the AOC down on her head. She called the Middlesex County Prosecutor, with whom she had shared an office back in the day, and by the next status conference date, Mr. Tough Guy was gone and a more reasonable prosecutor was sitting in his place. The backlog of cases was quickly resolved.

During my time with Judge Markashevsky, I had the opportunity of meeting one of the top defense attorneys in the state, a so-called Mob lawyer from Newark who was trying a case before the judge. Since he knew I appeared before her all the time, he had questions for me and I was happy to help him out. During one of his trial days, he invited me to have lunch with him, an invitation I readily accepted. We went to a Chinese restaurant right across the street from the courthouse. It was a memorable lunch, with my new acquaintance telling me all sorts of interesting stories about the Mafia defendants he'd represented. When our meals finally came out, he said to me, "Try a dumpling, John. I had them yesterday and they were the best I have ever eaten." I had a big plate of steaming General Tso's chicken in front of me that I couldn't wait to dig into, but I didn't want to be rude so I grabbed my fork and leaned over and took one of his dumplings and popped it into my mouth.

The lawyer watched me chewing for a minute or two and then asked, "How is it?" In truth, the dumplings weren't going to bring any Michelin stars to the place, but I said, "Delicious." Five minutes later, he said, "You know, I had this Tai Peng Mei Fun a couple of days ago, and it was excellent. I want you to try it."

By this point the General Tso's wasn't sitting too well, and I begged off. He looked at me and, while playing with his pinky ring, repeated in a serious voice, "I want you to try it, John."

Not wanting to piss off my new friend, I again leaned over and took a bite of his food. "What do you think? Is it all right?" he inquired. It tasted like cardboard, but not wanting to offend him I said, "Wow, I could be sitting on top of the Great Wall … this Tai Peng Mei Fun is like Chinese New Year in my mouth!"

"That's good, John," he said, watching me for another moment before starting to eat. Lunch continued for another 10 minutes or so, and when the check came, he grabbed it. I thanked him and he responded, "Fuhgeddaboudit." As we left the restaurant I was think-ing to myself, "What a guy."

About two months later, I came across a magazine profile of my lunch partner, a very entertaining article that touched upon many of his high profile cases. What really caught my attention, though, was a mention near the end of the story of how, about two years earlier, he'd been intentionally poisoned at a restaurant and nearly died.

What a guy!

I spent about three years working for the Middlesex County public defender's office, and during those years, I handled more than 20 jury trials and represented a thousand or more clients. I learned how to get things done. It was awesome.

Not long ago, I was reading an article in the *Wall Street Journal* about hiring attorneys. It mentioned that if you are charged criminally, you want to hire a former prosecutor because they make the best private defense attorneys. This is flat-out wrong. If it's a rinky-dink case where you are going to receive straight probation, then an ex-prosecutor is probably okay, but if you are in real trouble and need somebody to fight for you, you had better get a former public defender. Prosecutors almost always have the mindset that everyone is guilty. As soon as you walk in the door to hire a former prosecutor, he or she is thinking that you are guilty. Somebody who comes from a public defender's office, on the other hand, will at the very least give you the benefit of the doubt, and, if you *are* guilty, they won't care. In addition, prosecutors spend their time working for the government convicting people. Public defenders spend their time getting guilty people off, and they learn a hundred tricks along the way. There is no comparison. If your back is against the wall, you're better off with an old, long-haired hippie public defender in khakis and a tweed jacket than with an ex-prosecutor in a perfectly tailored suit.

I loved being in the Middlesex County public defender's office. The best part about it was the cast of characters. It was like the "Island of Misfit Toys" meets the "Dirty Dozen." Now don't for a moment think I'm being judgmental, because I was as much a misfit as any attorney working out of that office. I was a conservative Republican surrounded by a bunch of lefties in the ultimate lefty profession. Talk about being a fish out of water! (As to personal quirks, just talk to my wife.) But I really liked the people who worked at the public defender's office.

While I've singled out Dr. Pfeiffer and "Red" Barker, all of my fellow Middlesex attorneys had interesting backgrounds and idiosyncrasies. One lawyer had a knack for summing up complex topics with pithy comments. On the subject of police testimony, he'd say, "They all lie and everyone knows it." On the matter of confessions, "Fish only get caught when they open their mouths." Another public defender often feigned poor hearing. Once, while I was sitting with her outside a courtroom, a prosecutor who was trying a case against her walked up and jokingly said, "Sandy, how come you only have a hearing problem when a witness says something that's good for your case? When that one witness said he didn't recognize your client, you asked him to speak louder and repeat it, several times, but when the next witness ID'd him, it seemed your hearing was just fine." We all laughed.

The best lawyer I ever knew worked at the public defender's office. His name was Marty Matlaga, and the man was a trial machine. When I met him, he was approaching his 100th criminal jury trial and was, as I recall, on a winning streak of 10 consecutive not guilty verdicts—a remarkable number, since most defense attorneys are lucky to win one-third of their cases. Extremely successful high profile attorneys in private practice, who have the luxury of picking and choosing which cases they will try, may win 50 percent of the time. But here's Marty, taking all sorts of crappy public defender cases to trial and winning almost all of them—and I'm not talking about cases where you get not guilty verdicts on the serious charges but go down on the lesser offenses. I mean straight, run-the-field not guilty verdicts.

Defense lawyers have differing definitions of a "win." For some,
a split verdict is a win. For others, keeping the jury out for over an
hour before it comes back with a guilty verdict is a win. A while
back, the Mercer County prosecutor's office liked to say it had a
conviction rate at trial of 90 percent, which sounded impressive
until you got behind the numbers. The office considered any conviction in an indictment as a win. Thus, if a defendant was charged
with a triple homicide and was declared not guilty of all three murders but convicted on a fourth degree weapons offense, it was
chalked up as a win. Marty's standard was much higher: It was only
a win if he walked his client out the door after the verdict.

When it came to trial advocacy, Marty had it. Of course, you can
never define "it," a rare quality that you know when you see it. Kenny
Weiner was a great lawyer, but he would lose cases; he didn't quite
have "it." In my career, I've seen only two lawyers other than Marty
who possessed the elusive "it," and they are not the attorneys you
might think of. One has a small practice, and the other is a public
defender in another county. Having "it" doesn't necessarily result in
a lot of wealthy clients or a high-profile career.

Marty Matlaga had a real connection with juries; they just loved
him. It was easy to see why. He was—and is—a pretty big guy, six
foot one or better, and his cowboy boots and full head of hair make
him seem even taller. When he walked into a courtroom, he owned
it. Whether it was a status conference for a fourth degree offense or
a murder trial, he just had the presence. And when it came to advo-
cating for his client, he was always respectful but never took shit
from any judge. Some judges accepted Marty on his terms, while
others made no secret of their contempt for his approach. Marty
couldn't care less what anyone else thought.

When it came to dressing, Marty was unusual. He rarely wore a suit, even at trial. He usually dressed in khakis and a tweed jacket or blazer. What really made Marty stand apart, though, was his tie. He almost always wore the same tie: light blue with a picture of Elmo on it, as in Elmo from *Sesame Street*. It was bizarre. You would think a juror would look at that crazy tie with the big red fuzzy thing on it and just assume the lawyer was a nut and tune out anything he said. Not the case. For whatever reason, the tie worked. Marty was the gunslinger in the Elmo tie.

In addition to possessing natural talent, Marty worked extremely hard; nobody knew a file better than he did. Tom told me he once took a friend to the public defender's office on a Saturday night around 8:00 PM to show him where he worked. Inside, they found Marty preparing for a trial. (And, remember, he was a *government* employee!)

The Middlesex public defender's office had a great sense of camaraderie. The secretary at the front desk controlled an office-wide intercom system, and whenever a trial went the right way for one of the attorneys, she'd put on her best sportscaster's voice and announce that so-and-so "got a not guilty verdict!" The office would erupt into cheers. On those occasions when I heard "John Hartmann got a not guilty verdict!" and the ensuing acclamation, it was the best feeling in the world—like Rocky Balboa must have felt after he laid out Mr. T. (All that was missing was "Eye of the Tiger" playing in the background.) Far more often, however, I would be sitting in another lawyer's office or in the library when the announcement came that "Marty got another not guilty!" After cheering along with the rest, I'd pop into Marty's office to congratulate him and talk about his latest triumph. It was always something special.

Not long after I left the public defender's office in Middlesex in 2002, a judge complained so much about Marty Matlaga that the public defender bigwigs in Trenton moved him to another county, no doubt to curry favor with the powers that be. After a short while, he quit and opened his own practice, but when he asked to be assigned cases, Trenton actually blackballed him from the pool list. Imagine that—one of the best trial attorneys in the state, unable to get assigned a simple drug case. The aging liberals running the New Jersey public defender's office were all gung ho about defending people's rights, but apparently not where assigning an effective lawyer might get in the way of advancing their own careers. The poor and marginalized would just have to make do with a less experienced attorney.

The lawyers weren't the only interesting people I met while working in the Middlesex County court system. One of my responsibilities while in Middlesex was to represent people for violations of probation. If a defendant is placed on probation, the State really doesn't require much. He has to report regularly to a probation officer (PO), stay off drugs, find a little work, not commit any new offenses, and pay up to $1,200 in fines over a three- to five-year period (about $33 a month in the worst case scenario). Some probationers couldn't meet even these unexacting standards, and violations were commonplace for such offenses as having "dirty" urine, not reporting as scheduled, or failing to gain or maintain at least part-time employment.

In Middlesex County, violations of probation are heard on Friday morning. The public defender meets his client (assuming he shows) at court and then talks to the PO to try to work out a deal. If a deal is struck, it is presented to the prosecutor, who almost always agrees to it. The defendant is then brought before the judge, who typically yells at him as though he is a wayward child and then "reluctantly" reinstates him on probation, hopefully to violate no more. If the matter cannot be worked out then, there is a hearing where the PO testifies and the judge determines by the preponderance of the evidence (not beyond a reasonable doubt) whether there was a violation. Judges always find violations, and if you go to a hearing, you are going to lose.

Working the probation circuit, I had the opportunity to meet Mike the Probation Officer. Mike was about five years older than me and a Rutgers University graduate. We spent a lot of our Friday mornings together talking about cases, becoming pretty good friends in the process.

Our conversations would often turn to the philosophical. For instance, we wondered at the human condition, and how people who are facing jail time not only do unbelievably stupid things but repeat the same mistakes over and over again. After all, we opined, a lab rat learns after one or two attempts that if it tries to grab food that's being electrically charged it will receive a painful shock, and so stops trying. This lesson that a rat picks up in 10 seconds somehow escapes many a sorrowful probationer. I personally was amazed to discover that for a brief period of instant gratification, some probationers are apparently willing to face up to five years in state prison.

After listening to various probationers' lame stories on Friday mornings, week in and week out, Mike and I developed a little comic routine. It was called, "I got a better idea." Basically, it was a skit where I was an angel standing on the probationer's shoulder whispering into his ear and Mike was the devil standing on the other shoulder. The probationer would always listen to Mike.

Angel: "You have $125 in fines and three years to pay it off. Get a job and pay probation ten dollars a month."

Devil: "I got a better idea. Don't pay any fines and wait until your probation is violated; the day before your hearing hold up a gas station to get the cash."

Another example:

Angel: "You are going to be drug tested tomorrow and if you fail you are going to jail. Don't do any drugs today."

Devil: "I got a better idea. Smoke the biggest blunt you can find tonight. Drink two gallons of water in the morning to wash it out of your system. You'll be fine."

Or:

Angel: "Today is court. Get up early, dress well, and arrive 15 minutes before the doors open. Your PO said as long as you show up he will put you back on probation."

Devil: "I got a better idea. You had a late night. Sleep in."

You get the picture.

It was during this time as a per diem attorney that I tried the most bizarre case of my career. My client, whom we'll call Raul, was a very hard man and one scary dude. He was a little over six feet tall, tough and wiry, and wore his raven black hair in a big pompadour above his scarred and pockmarked face. Raul was Cuban and had served as a paratrooper in Fidel's army, fighting, among other places, in Angola, where he said he saw some "really bad shit." He also told me he'd been a Golden Gloves boxer in his home country; I had no reason not to believe him.

In the early 1990s, Raul had escaped Communist Cuba and come to America, where he quickly embraced capitalism and opened his own business in Perth Amboy selling drugs. When the cops busted into his house, they found three and a half ounces of cocaine in plain view on his kitchen table. But that wasn't all they found.

Raul was mad as a hatter—nothing that rose to a defense, mind you, just plain crazy. But I have represented a lot of crazy people in my life, and there was nothing unusual about the fact that Raul was nuts. What made this case surreal was that Raul practiced Santeria, otherwise known as White Magic. In fact, he was a Babalorisha, or priest, in the Santeria religion. When the police broke into his apartment, Raul was in the middle of a ceremony dressed in nothing but a pure white bathrobe. There were about 50 burning candles throughout the apartment and, amid the candles, along with the 100 grams of "blow" and the scantily clad Raul, were dozens of miniature statues of Catholic saints. It must have been quite a sight.

To make things even more interesting, there was a co-defendant in the case, a 50-year-old local Hispanic gentleman who was arrested in the apartment. When apprehended, he was fully clothed and had one small bag of cocaine on him. Clearly, he was a buyer and was only indicted for possession of a CDS (controlled dangerous substance). He was about five foot two, bald, swarthy, and fat, and had a big bushy mustache. His appearance immediately brought to mind Sancho Panza from *The Man of La Mancha*, and the co-defendants became known around court as Don Quicaine and Sancho.

As cases go, it was a dog. It was my client's apartment, and when the cops arrived, the kitchen table was covered with more white powder than a German grandmother needs for rolling out strudel. He might as well have been doing an Al Pacino impersonation from the last scene in *Scarface*: "You fuck with Raul, you fuck with the best, you cock-a-roach!" This guy was going down, and going down hard. The fact that he had no criminal record would save him from spending the next decade in jail, but it was inconceivable that he'd get less than a five-year sentence with a three-year stip if he went to trial. That's why Raul needed to take the State's relatively generous offer for a little over one year in jail.

I'm usually pretty good at explaining the facts of a case to a client, but Raul didn't want to hear any of it—he was going to trial. In fact, Raul would never listen to a word I was saying; he would just talk and talk about trying the case. Finally, I went to see him at the workhouse before we signed a trial memo. After listening to him talk complete bullshit for one hour, I was willing to say anything to get out of there. Hell, I would have rather had a root canal with no pain medication than listen to Raul for five more minutes. He finally said, "When I boxed, before I went into the ring, I needed to know I had a 90 percent chance of winning. With 90 percent I would fight. Do we have a 90 percent chance of winning?"

For the only time in my career, I lied to a client about such an important issue. "Raul, our chances are at least 80 percent," I answered, throwing out a random high number. (On a good day, they were really about 2 percent.) "Fine," he responded, "we will fight."

Before the trial, I had offered to get my client some clothes for court. "No, thank you," he said, having seen how the public defender's office dressed its charges. He was going to get his own outfit. Trial day came and he was brought to court—dressed like a mime. But it was worse than that: Rather than a mime's shirt with standard black and white stripes, his had purple stripes to match his incredibly tight (I mean *Robert Plant* tight) purple jeans.

For me, a bright spot in the case was that one of my best friends, a lawyer named David Oakely, was representing Raul's co-defendant—Sancho, that is. Outside of that, the case didn't go well. A number of Perth Amboy detectives testified about what they had found in Raul's abode during their investigation. Throughout the trial, Raul sat next to me, his head bent over into his hand, sinking lower and lower into his chair after each witness. By the time the State's last witness testified, his face was perpendicular to the counsel table.

During the testimony, I'd heard Raul mumbling to himself in Spanish. I had no idea what he was talking about since about the only Spanish I use is *no carcel* (no jail), *no dinero, no abogado* (no money, no lawyer), and *cojones* (testicles). But one of the detectives who testified spoke fluent Spanish, and during a break in the case, he came up to me and said, "You better watch out. Your client is mumbling spells against you, and I know this guy. He can be pretty dangerous."

"Great," I thought, picturing the headline in tomorrow's paper: "Local Lawyer Killed by Babalorisha After Verdict."

For no particular reason, the co-defendant decided to testify on his own behalf and stated that he never had any cocaine in his pockets. Because he was Spanish-speaking, an interpreter was used. I really didn't have any questions for him, but decided to show Raul I was trying before his hex turned me into a chicken. My cross-examination went as follows:

"So, before you went to the apartment you were drinking beer?" I asked.

"*Si*," the witness responded.

Not knowing where I was going with this, I needed to stall for time so I asked another question of no importance.

"How many beers?"

"Twenty-three."

"*What*?" I'm thinking to myself—*nobody* admits to drinking 23 beers; it is always one or two, maybe three. I've had driving-while-intoxicated clients who blew three times the legal limit and are dying of cirrhosis of the liver say they had two beers when in actuality it was more like two bottles of vodka. Completely taken aback by the answer, I asked him to confirm that he'd had 23 beers. "*Si*," he said. Not knowing what to ask next, my brilliant cross-examination continued as follows:

"What type of beer were you drinking?"

"Budweiser."

Searching for a line of questioning, I probed:

"The King of Beers?"

"*Siiii*."

At this point I thought to myself, well, I'm out of ideas, and so announced, "No further questions, Your Honor." A scene from *Inherit the Wind* it was not.

The jury went out at 3:00 PM on a Friday. At 3:45, they told the sheriff's officers that they had a verdict. At 4:15, all the parties were at the counsel table and the jury came in. The chorus from a Lynyrd Skynyrd song was running through my head: "Give me three steps, give me three steps, mister, give me three steps to the door. Give me three steps, give me three steps, mister, and you'll never see me no more." I felt certain that as soon as the word "guilty" was uttered, Raul was going to go medieval on me.

"Ladies and gentlemen of the jury, have you reached a verdict?"

"Yes."

"And is that verdict unanimous?"

"Yes."

At this point, I was behind Raul slipping quietly to the door.

"How do you find the defendant—guilty or not guilty of possession of CDS with intent to distribute?"

Okay, I think to myself, I am ready to duck and run.

"Not guilty."

"Say what?"

The jury continued, delivering a verdict of not guilty on all counts. Raul turned to me, grinning from ear to ear. He told me that he never doubted me and that I am beautiful, and for the first and only time in my life, I found myself being kissed on the lips by another man. (Of course, it did nothing for me.)

Now, before you decide that this case proves the mystical power of Santeria, I'll point out two factors that, in hindsight, helped us win the case. First, during jury selection, a prospective juror asked for a side bar. He informed us that he had been on a jury once before in a drug case where the defendant was convicted. He then said he had read in the paper a couple of months later what the ultimate sentence was for the defendant and had been disgusted by its severity. In other words, he was never going to convict a defendant on a drug charge. For some unfathomable reason, the prosecutor did not knock him off.

Second, the jury got the case after three o'clock on a Friday. Most jurors don't like to come back for a second week of service, so there was every incentive for them to resolve the case quickly. With one juror refusing to find anyone guilty, the other jurors quickly caved in. In fact, we found out later from someone who knew one of the jurors that 11 had voted not guilty almost immediately once they realized what they were up against. The lone holdout was a woman who, coincidently, was the only African American on the jury. She held out for half an hour, then, realizing she was not going to prevail, voted not guilty, saying, "You're all crazy, but if you don't care, *I* don't care."

It just goes to show that when you go to trial, you never really know what a jury may do.

Raul may have been guilty, and you may find it a miscarriage of justice that he walked. However, I can assure you that for every Raul who may have gotten away with a crime, there is one innocent person sitting in jail. I will offer two examples.

It was during my struggles with Raul that I was assigned my first murder case. The facts were relatively simple. Four individuals drove to a rival drug dealer's house, and one of the passengers went inside and put a bullet in the competition's head. Then they all left. A short while later, the driver was pulled over for a minor infraction. They weren't arrested that night, but after some good detective work, one thing led to another and they were all charged about a month later. I represented the driver. (As a quick aside, I've seen many a criminal enterprise fall apart because the weak link in a group was the driver; the takeaway here is the importance of having a dependable "wheel man" on any job that needs one. I cannot reiterate this point enough: Always have a good wheel man.)

This case was pretty straightforward. My client pled guilty to aggravated manslaughter and received a decent offer of 12 years in exchange for testifying against the shooter. What was interesting about the case was that before my client and his three co-defendants were arrested, the police had charged another person. Even more remarkable, that person had given what is known as a "false confession." And I don't mean he said, "Yeah, I wacked that guy, charge me." He gave a five-page, single-spaced statement going into detail about how he killed the victim. He explained why he did it, how he drove there, how he shot the man, and what he did with the handgun afterward. He gave it all up.

The only problem was that the confession was a complete fabrication, and, when it was determined that someone else did the killing, the State had to jump through hoops to dismiss the charges against the innocent party. If it weren't for a serious and honest detective working this case, an innocent man would be doing life and the killer would be free.

I had a similar case about a year earlier. My client had been charged with burglary, and it appeared to be an airtight case. Two independent witnesses had identified him, and a co-defendant had given a statement against him. The burglary was caught on video and while the video evidence was not conclusive, the felon sure looked like my client.

In fact, the only problem with the State's case was that my client *didn't* do it, and he had an alibi they couldn't get around: He'd been incarcerated in another county prison at the time of the burglary. This man wasn't guilty, but I have no doubt that if he hadn't been in jail when the crime was committed, he would have been convicted.

In many areas of life, the principle that things tend to "even out" may have something going for it. But the way I see it, the "even out" theory isn't so great if you're behind bars for a crime you never committed.

6

HAVE GUN, WILL TRAVEL

I was sitting at my conference table, talking to Robin. Robin and I are great friends, even though she thinks I'm neurotic and I find her ungodly loud. She calls me her "office husband." I call her my "office wife." Except for my real wife, I don't know a better person than Robin. About six years ago, I received a call from Robin out of the clear blue; she wanted to discuss a criminal trial she was about to start. I had met her once or twice and thought she seemed nice, if a little obnoxious. It seemed she hadn't tried a criminal case in 15 years and was looking for a couple of pointers. She asked a few other attorneys for advice on whom she might approach and was apparently told that I knew my way around a courtroom. We met at my office to discuss her case, and as it turned out, she had just gone out on her own and was looking for office space. I had office space to spare, one thing led to another, and we have been bullshitting together ever since.

What were we talking about in my office on that particular afternoon? We were not talking about strategy in some big homicide case. Nor were we talking about a new Supreme Court case or a change in the law. We were talking about something far more important: getting clients to pay, or, as we sometimes say, "Having Mr. Green pay a visit."

Some people are surprised to hear that this is a big problem for defense attorneys, since a lawyer is often the only thing standing between a defendant and a jail cell, but after all, you are dealing with criminals. What you don't get up front, you may not get at all.

It is not necessarily that clients don't want to pay, but once you enter an appearance and become the attorney of record in a case, it is very difficult to get out, and they seem to instinctively know this. Other bills start coming in and the attorney's lands at the bottom of the pile, in part because, unlike some other creditors, we can't turn off anyone's electric or water. Sometimes I don't feel like a lawyer so much as a collection agent, a collection agent specializing in litigation.

So the conversation started when I complained to Robin that I had not received a check that a client had assured me he'd mailed a week ago. The week had passed but there was no sign of "Mr. Green."

"Robin, have you ever noticed how envelopes with money in them just travel slower?" I began. "When people mail a letter it takes one, maybe two days to arrive. When someone sends me a bill, it arrives in one day, guaranteed. But when people put a check in an envelope, it always seems to take an extra week."

"Yeah, the post office must deliver letters with money in them by Pony Express," she said. "They also flat out lose a lot of letters with money in them. I was just reminding a client yesterday about a payment, and she swore on her mother's grave she'd mailed the money order 10 days ago. Funny, I don't seem to lose any junk mail, but letters with checks just disappear. Which reminds me, guess who I am representing tonight?"

"I'll bite. Who?" I asked, knowing it would be an amusing answer.

"Mr. I-Get-Paid-On-Friday."

"No way, Robin. I thought you were done with that guy."

"I know, I'm an idiot," she said. "Just shoot me."

Mr. I-Get-Paid-On-Friday was originally a client of mine. He wasn't really a bad person, just a drunk—the suck-back-on-nail-polish-remover type of drunk. When he hired me initially, he had been busted for driving while intoxicated and under suspension. I managed to jump through some hoops and do a good job for him and keep him out of jail. I also sat down with him one day in my office and had a long talk with him about his drinking. Now, usually I don't have conversations with clients about their substance abuse for two reasons. First, it's none of my business; I was hired as a lawyer, not as a priest or counselor. Second, there's almost no chance a client is going to take my advice in such matters anyway. However, I had a good rapport with this man and felt I could talk to him openly and perhaps make a difference. He had a young son, and the boy's mother was addicted to something harder than hooch.

Well, I had not heard from Mr. I-Get-Paid-On-Friday for about six months after my solo intervention when out of the blue he called me. He said I had changed his life, that he had been stone cold sober ever since we talked, and I have to say his gratitude left me with a really warm, fuzzy feeling.

Addictions are a hard thing to overcome, and Mr. I-Get-Paid-On-Friday's sobriety lasted about two more months before he started hitting the bottle and getting into trouble again. He had always been good about paying in the past (he hadn't yet earned his nickname), but now the payments became infrequent. Any time I mentioned to him that he owed me money, he'd say, "I get paid on Friday. I'll see you then." I might point out to him that it was Monday and that he'd been paid three days earlier, and how about *not* spending the week-end swimming in the "drunk tank" so he could drop some "frog skins" on me. It had no effect. "I get paid on Friday" was his inevitable response.

Needless to say, Friday would come around and he would not answer his phone and he sure as hell wouldn't call me. The last time

I represented him, he should have left the court in cuffs through the steel doors in the back, but thanks to a strong defense, he left with me through the glass doors out front. As we were walking out to our cars—his license was suspended but he was still driving—I said to him, "Let me guess, you get paid on Friday."

"That's right, John," he nodded, "I get paid on Friday."

The next time Mr. I-Get-Paid-On-Friday got in trouble and called me, I referred him to Robin, though I warned her to get her money up front. He started off paying her and then stopped, assuring her every time he saw her that he got paid on Friday. Friday would come and, true to form, he wouldn't answer his cell phone—I guess he was too busy working. I asked Robin why she continued to represent him when she knew she was going to get beat.

"I said you still owe me from the last two cases," she sighed. "But when he asked me to do it for his son, what could I say?" I'm more hardnosed than Robin, so I said, "How about *no*?"

Knowing I had to get back to work, I jokingly asked, "Hey Robin, what is the sweetest phrase in the English language?" We had discussed this issue at great length a few years earlier and come up with the answer. Without missing a beat she said, "Is cash okay?"

"You got it, Robin!"

Welcome to my world.

The great thing about opening your own law practice is that it's about the easiest business to start. There is no other business I know of that's cheaper to get going (not counting the cost of law school). You need an office, a desk, some file cabinets, a phone, a copier, and a computer with a printer. A conference table would also be nice but it's not critical. You probably *should* purchase legal insurance. In all, you can start a law practice for under $5,000. Try opening a restaurant with $5,000.

Sitting in your new office, behind your new desk, waiting for your new phone to ring, you might wonder what to expect. If you are going to do criminal law, you'd better be ready for a lot of different things. But one thing you shouldn't expect is that your practice will bear any resemblance to what you've seen on *Law and Order*. That show may be entertaining fiction, but that's all it is—fiction. There is nothing remotely accurate about it, at least from the point of view of the criminal defense attorney. My biggest beef is that almost every episode has a slick criminal defense attorney filing a motion of some sort before the case is even indicted. "Here you go, McCoy," the attorney says, handing the *über* DA a blue envelope. "My client's rights were trampled, the statement is out." Or, "McCoy, the search was bad and the jury will never see the gun." Two scenes later, McCoy and the defense attorney are talking to the judge, in chambers, as he waters his plants. "I agree with defense counsel," the judge says. "The statement is out."

So there you have it—poor McCoy, crucified on the cross of the Fourth and Fourteenth Amendments, sandbagged by some liberal judge, barely holding his case together. But all of a sudden, with four minutes to go in the trial, the otherwise brilliant and high-priced defense attorney decides to commit malpractice by sticking his client on the stand. Within 30 seconds, McCoy has the defendant babbling like a newborn, giving it all up. McCoy grabs victory out of the jaws of defeat, and all is right with the world again.

This scenario is complete bullshit. There is a rule of thumb in criminal law that the chances of winning any motion are proportional to the seriousness of the case. If your client is caught with a couple bags of dope and even if convicted is getting probation, then maybe you can get the case thrown out on a motion. But if there is a body in the case, you are not winning anything. There is almost no way a judge is going to throw out a statement or suppress evidence in a murder case. Anything short of a video showing two detectives beating your client senseless with phone books and you are going to lose. Hell, even with the phone book beat-down, the statement may still come in. All the detectives have to say is, "Your Honor, we were just trying to help the defendant find a lawyer in the yellow pages and he fell into the phone book … ten times."

I can hear the judge's ruling now: "I find the detectives' testimony credible, and I find Mr. Hartmann's argument to be without merit. In fact, I find his argument bordering on frivolous." No judge wants to be on the front page of the local paper with the headline "Looney Liberal Judge Lets Killer Walk" or, even worse, be lambasted on *The O'Reilly Factor*. Their thinking is, by and large, let the appellate division make the tough decisions. You want justice? Maybe you can find it down Market Street at the Hughes Justice Complex, where the appellate division sits.

If you are young and have your heart set on becoming a criminal defense attorney, for practice I suggest becoming a Kansas City Royals fan, because it will get you used to losing. In fact, you had better get used to having your head handed to you on a platter on a regular basis. I had one murder case where I kept count: 32 motions, 32 denials. Now, maybe some of my motions *should* have been denied, maybe even *most* of my motions should have been denied—but all 32 of them?

By the time we reached the twentieth consecutive denial, I thought my head was going to explode. Five denials later I mentioned that I had not won a motion and the judge actually said, "We are not keeping count." I responded, "I *am* keeping count, Your Honor, and that was 25 in a row!"

If you are the type of person who needs to win all the time—that is, if when you were 12 and your little brother was eight, you couldn't help running up the score 10–0 in one-on-one basketball, or if you were the kid whose favorite football team was always the one that just won the Super Bowl—then forget about becoming a defense lawyer. Be a *prosecutor*.

There is this misconception that prosecutors are great cross-examiners, a fallacy perpetrated by television. In most trials, prosecutors don't even have the opportunity to cross-examine witnesses. In fact, if you can say the words, "And then what happened?" you, too, can prosecute a double homicide. Call a witness, and just keep asking, "And then what happened?" and the judge will do the rest of the work. Most prosecutors couldn't get their own three-year-old to admit to taking the cookie out of the cookie jar, even with crumbs all over the child's face.

"Honey, I saw you take the cookie. You told your big sister you took the cookie. Half the cookie is in your hand. Now, baby, did you or did you not take the cookie?" The child's response: "No, Daddy, no take cookie," as she munches away.

Now contrast this with how a defense attorney is going to handle the case. First, he'll sit the child down in a chair and walk over to the cookie jar, and then he'll slowly come back and peer down at the child for 10 seconds. Next, he will say the child's name—not yell it but utter it with authority. The cookie culprit will immediately exclaim, "Sorry, Daddy, took cookie!"

Seriously, if you want to be a good cross-examiner—and learn some excellent parenting skills while you're at it—*defend* criminals, don't prosecute them.

One thing I learned early on in my practice was not to waste my time sitting around waiting for that big case to come through the door, the case where I'd have my Johnny Cochran moment and get somebody guilty as sin off with a cute little catchphrase like "If the glove doesn't fit, you must acquit." During one of my first trials, I was representing a young African American man accused of a home invasion robbery of a couple of Rutgers students. I was cross-examining the police officer who had arrested my client and noted that in the police report under "race" the suspect was identified as a "number two." I asked the officer about this and he stated that whites were listed as "ones," African Americans as "twos," Hispanics as "threes," and so on (Samoans were listed as "seventeens"). In the course of my summation, I came up with a nifty little rhyme decrying racial injustice: "They were looking for a number two, and any number two would do." I cringe today to think I actually said that to a jury, and in fact, it didn't work very well. We went down in flames. (Another lesson I learned during the same trial is that when the victim is testifying and a juror starts crying, it's a bad sign.)

In order to build a client base you have to hustle, there are no two ways about it. My advice is, first, to try to get on the pool list for the public defender's office. Next, contact established lawyers you know and ask them if they need any help. It might not pay a lot but it gets you into court. Get into court as much as possible, because once you start representing people (and assuming you get good results) you will earn repeat business and your clients will refer their friends and family to you. Yellow Pages and internet advertising can be very helpful; the rule of thumb is that for every dollar you spend on advertising, you'll get two back. However, the competition is fierce, with numerous lawyers following the same strategy (if you are looking to obtain the number "1-800-wasnt-me" don't bother—it's taken), and prospective clients who find you in the Yellow Pages are often shopping for the lowest price. (Of course, this is where keeping your expenses down is so important, because if someone is looking for a good deal, you can probably provide it.) So, yes—advertise, but realize it's no substitute for someone calling to say, "I was referred to you by my cousin and he says you were great." When that happens, chances are you're about to be hired.

You'll still need to close the deal, and that's where developing rapport comes in. When someone comes to your office to talk about possible representation, there are a number of simple things you can do to increase your chances of being retained. First, you must know what you are talking about. Prepare for the meeting by finding out what the individual has been charged with, and read the statute beforehand unless you already know it inside and out.

Second, sit and listen. Let the client tell you his or her side of the story and don't interrupt except to ask one or two clarifying questions.

Third, show some empathy. Take the approach that if the prosecutor is trying to screw the client, he's trying to screw you. Your mantra should be, "Whatsoever you do to the least of my clients, that is what you do unto me."

Fourth, explain what the charges mean and what the client is facing in terms of penalties. Never, *ever* talk about pleading guilty during the first meeting unless the client specifically asks you about a plea. Very few prospective clients are going to spend money just to have you plead them out—they want a fighter, not a pleader. If necessary you can say, "We don't plead guilty unless we *are* guilty," but not until at least the second meeting.

Finally, never talk money until you have thoroughly discussed the case. After a positive first meeting, it's likely the prospective client will want to hire you, but if they can't afford you, so be it. Worst case scenario, they'll go home thinking you were decent enough to talk to them, and if they get in trouble again, or a friend does, you might get a phone call down the line. Just be sure to hand them a bunch of your business cards when they leave.

When I first started out, a very experienced attorney gave me some great advice about building a client base. He told me that the key to success was to get into an arrangement with a bail bondsman.

People are entitled to bail if charged with a criminal offense—it's a right that is actually enshrined in the United States Constitution (I think Ben Franklin and Alexander Hamilton knew the importance of bail after a night of carousing). If you are charged with a crime in New Jersey, three things can happen. If it is a relatively minor charge, you'll be given a summons, which means there is no detainer; you are "released on your own recognizance" (ROR). For other offenses, a bail amount is set that you'll have to post, designed to assure your return to court. Bail can range from $2,500 for less serious offenses all the way up to $2,000,000 for murder; it usually falls in the $10,000 to $100,000 range. For fourth and third degree offenses, you may have a 10 percent option, which means you only have to put down 10 percent of the bail amount to get out of jail. So, for instance, if your bail is $30,000 with a 10 percent option, you'll have to post $3,000 with the court. If there is no 10 percent option, you'll either have to put the entire amount of the bail down (which is rarely done) or hire a bail bondsman.

A bail bondsman will keep 10 percent of the bail as his fee. Again, using the example of the $30,000 bail, you'll pay the bondsman $3,000. If the bondsman thinks you have the money, he will typically ask for his fee up front, saying it is required by the courts. In actuality, you can get by on paying him half of the 10 percent (or less) and working out a payment schedule for the balance. In addition, you usually have to provide two signers who will agree to cover the bond in the event you skip town. The signers need to have verifiable jobs and preferably some property.

The bail bonds business is quite competitive. Look in any local Yellow Pages and you will find at least one such business. Inevitably, there will be AA Bail Bonds followed by AAA Bail Bonds, perhaps even followed by AAAA Bail Bonds (I have never seen AAAAA Bail Bonds, but I'd bet there's one out there). In the Trenton area alone you have, among others, Absolute Bail Bonds, AA Bail Bonds, ABC Bail Bonds, Bandit Bail Bonds (I can't wait to give my money to a company called Bandit), Blaze Bail Bonds, Capital City Bail Bonds, Freedom Bail Bonds, 1 Stop Bail Bonds, and Quick Release Bail Bonds. Some of these companies are well established, others are fly-by-night. The latter sort hit a city with guns blazing, bailing everyone out for the smallest amount down. I have seen people with $100,000 bail get out of jail for as little as $3,000. For a year or so the good times roll, but once defendants start skipping town and bails are forfeited, the Department of Insurance steps in and closes the bail bonds business down. Most pop up under a new name somewhere else in the state, and the cycle starts all over again.

One day, not long after I'd started working in Judge Markashevsky's courtroom, a young man in a suit walked up to me while I was standing by the elevators on the fifth floor of the Middlesex Courthouse. He extended his hand, introduced himself as Derek, and then handed me his card. It read "Capital City Bail Bonds" and had a caricature of an inmate with a gigantic foot kicking a hole through a jail house wall.

I told Derek I liked the drawing, and he explained that he'd designed it himself, inspired by the back cover of the Grateful

Dead's *Europe '72* album. I told him I'd been to a few Dead shows, and he said, "Me, too—about 150 of them. The last one I was supposed to go to was in Portland, but Jerry died about two weeks earlier."

At this point, Derek started to choke up a little, so I patted him on the shoulder and said, "Sorry about Jerry, man, that was a shame." Jerry Garcia had died in 1995, and I met Derek in 1998. This guy was a *real* Dead Head—not a *faux* Dead Head like me.

Derek and I became fast friends and remain so today. I was in his wedding and he was in mine. As it turned out, besides digging the Dead, we were both fans of the Philadelphia Eagles and we soon started meeting up for the Sunday games. Today, the Eagles play in a beautiful stadium called Lincoln Financial Field, which offers every amenity you could ask for while enjoying football on a Sunday afternoon. It also costs about a zillion bucks a ticket. Back when Derek and I were going, the "Iggles" played at Veterans Stadium, informally known as "the Vet." The Vet was built in 1971 for both baseball and football. It was a foul-smelling, poorly designed edifice, but at least a guy could afford seats in the 700 level.

Attending an Eagles game is really just an excuse to get drunk. You show up a couple of hours before the game to tailgate and drink beer. About half an hour before kickoff, you walk over to the stadium, where along with thousands of other green-clad drunken idiots you are herded inside, like cattle being led into the slaughterhouse. Eventually you arrive at your seats, which are so high up you can barely see the field. Then it's time to hit the concession stands, where the *privilege* of buying a semi-cold Miller Lite will run you over seven dollars. The Vet was most definitely not an Irish-friendly place.

I have a particularly vivid memory of one game I went to with Derek. For whatever reason, neither of us was drinking. It was a beautiful fall day and an exciting game that we actually watched all the way through. After a nail-biting Eagles win, Derek said, "Maybe we're better off not drinking at these games," a statement to which I readily agreed. Two weeks later, we were both half-in-the-bag by kickoff time.

The "City of Brotherly Love" has the reputation of having the most unruly fans this side of Glasgow, and as an observer of the Philly faithful for more than three decades, I think the reputation is deserved. These fans are loud, obnoxious, cruel, and heartless. Eagles fans, in particular, got so out of hand at the Vet that the City of Philadelphia set up a temporary municipal court at every home game. People who wear opposition team jerseys to an Eagles game are inevitably and loudly jeered as "assholes," or worse. You could be a nun, but if you're wearing a Redskins cap over your habit at an Eagles–Skins game, you are going to be verbally abused.

The only exception to this rule I have personally witnessed was at an Eagles–Raiders game at the Vet. Before the game, a group of Oakland fans were tailgating in the parking lot and it looked like a Pagans convention. Nobody said "boo" to them for fear of a violent beating at the hands of pumped-up six foot five bikers brandishing tire irons and chains. What I learned that day is that while Eagles fans can be drunk and stupid, they aren't completely suicidal.

Derek has sent me a number of cases over the years, and when I have clients who need bail done, I always refer them to Derek, knowing that they will get good, professional service rather than getting ripped off. (If you are looking for a dependable bail bonds-man, call Derek at 609-396-8888.)

About 10 years ago, I read a book titled *Lincoln*, for which author David Herbert Donald was awarded the Pulitzer Prize. This is the definitive one-volume biography of America's16th president. Now,

everyone knows that Lincoln was our greatest president. He pre-
served the Union. He freed the slaves. But what most people don't
know is that before he became president, "the Great Emancipator"
was one bad-ass street lawyer. When he came before a jury, the man
was hell on wheels. He hustled files, argued down judges, and beat
murder raps for clients with the best of them. In fact, of the great
lawyers of all time—including Cicero, Daniel Webster, Daniel "The
Liberator" O'Connell, Clarence Darrow, and F. Lee Bailey—
Honest Abe may have been the best.

   In an early section of his book, Donald writes about Lincoln's
legal career. Lincoln practiced law from the 1830s until his election
to the Presidency in 1860. The law firm of Lincoln and Herndon
was located in Springfield, Illinois, the state capital, but for a good
part of the year Lincoln would ride the circuit with other lawyers
and judges. This judicial caravan would travel the backwoods of
Central Illinois, moving from one town to the next, setting up courts
and arguing cases. Among his peers, Lincoln was a standout. As
Donald described his technique:

> In court he rarely raised objections when opposing coun-
> sel introduced evidence. According to Leonard Swett,
> the young Bloomington lawyer who traveled the circuit
> with Lincoln, "he would say he 'reckoned' it would be
> fair to let this in …" But this, Swett noted, did not mean
> that he yielded essentials: "What he was so blandly giv-
> ing away was what he couldn't get and keep." Many a
> rival lawyer was lulled into complacency as Lincoln
> conceded, say, six out of seven points in argument, only
> to discover that the whole case turned on the seventh
> point. "Any man who took Lincoln for a simple-minded

man," Swett concluded, "would very soon wake up with his back in a ditch." (David Herbert Donald, *Lincoln* [New York: Simon & Schuster, 1995], 149)

Abe Lincoln, doing Evidence the right way and cleaning opposing counsel's clock.

Awesome.

Lincoln practiced law in a very different time. It boggles my mind to think that he could function without copiers, phones, fax machines, or computers. Hell, he didn't even have a typewriter; everything had to be written out and copied by hand. In many ways, though, what Lincoln did in the 1830s and '40s is the same as what I and a hundred thousand other American lawyers do today. We travel the circuit.

When you think of a criminal defense attorney, you might visualize a flamboyant, elderly lawyer defending drug kingpins or mobsters in state or federal court. In actuality, the spectrum of case types most of us handle is extreme, anywhere from speeding tickets to murder cases. In fact, a large part of our practice is spent defending people in municipal court—in individual towns rather than at the county level—for motor vehicle violations and disorderly persons offenses. Working municipal court cases is simpler and, I think, preferable to working in Superior Court. While you won't be paid as much, you can usually resolve a case in one or two court appearances, and there's less pressure because the penalties are not nearly as severe. My most interesting municipal court case occurred in the rural municipality of West Amwell Township. My client was charged with "Possession of a Black Bear with Intent to Sell." The case involved a couple of hunters, a pickup truck, a late night, too much beer, a bad idea, and one very pissed-off bear. I'll have to leave it at that.

Lawyers, like great white sharks, are territorial, and we usually focus about 90 percent of our time on the same courts. A couple of times a month we may get out of our comfort zone, but by and large, we go to the same courts and see the same judges or prosecutors on a weekly or biweekly basis. I might be driving a car rather than riding a horse, and I might be fueled by Starbucks coffee instead of back country "rot gut" but I am basically doing what Lincoln did 160 years ago. On Monday mornings, I'm in Superior Court. In the afternoon, I might go to Hamilton Municipal Court, and in the evening, Ewing and East Windsor Courts are in session. On Tuesdays, there's Lawrence followed by Robbinsville Court in the evening. On Wednesdays, it's Plainsboro or Ewing again in the morning, and then West Windsor Court in the afternoon and evening. Thursday is usually a day for Superior Court in the morning, followed by Hamilton or Trenton Municipal Court in the afternoon. Friday is mainly reserved for State Court, though a case will sometimes take me to Trenton Municipal Court in the morning.

Add in a few additional courts you'll need to get to in a typical week and your schedule fills up very quickly. As a result, once you've established your practice, it's challenging to find enough office time to return phone calls, prepare and send correspondence, meet with clients and potential clients, and write motions and briefs. (I have no idea what I'd do without my Blackberry.) Fortunately, there's the weekend. A few uninterrupted hours at your desk on Saturday equates to an entire day in the office during the work week.

As you start building your client base, you'll find all types of people walking through your door, from career criminals to soccer moms to businessmen with Ivy League educations. The most responsible person you know can make that one big mistake, like drinking a little too much with friends and then getting behind the wheel of a car. Most of the individuals I represent are young, relatively speaking, but I've represented people of all ages, races, and backgrounds. In the process, I've learned that generalizations usually don't hold up—with the one exception that sex offenders are almost always Dallas Cowboys fans. I can't explain this phenomenon, but the next time you hear a Dallas fan say "How about them boys?" don't assume he's talking about his football team.

Many of the people you end up representing need your services because they have no sense. Human beings will do the craziest things. Let me give you just one modest example of the insanity defense lawyers must deal with; namely, how clients dress for court. The average person who knows he is about to appear before a judge will give some thought to his appearance. If he doesn't have a suit, he'll put on a jacket and tie and a decent pair of pants. There are, however, a number of shocking exceptions.

Now, I'm not the least bit surprised to see a defendant wander late into court wearing a T-shirt and shorts, but some wardrobe choices just blow my mind. I have seen people go before a judge in T-shirts featuring the image of Al Capone or Al Pacino as Scarface, emblazoned with the words "Public Enemy Number One." I have seen larger-than-life visages of Biggie Smalls and Tupac Shakur adorning the garb of the accused, begging the question, *What is wrong with people?*

Another common fashion *faux pas* that the criminal sect falls prey to are ridiculously baggy pants. I once had a juvenile client who sported a particularly baggy pair. For whatever reason, when we went to court, this budding genius didn't wear a belt. We were called before the judge and my client was standing next to me with his hands in his pockets, fidgeting, desperately trying to keep his pants up. Having your hands in your pockets is seen by many judges as a sign of disrespect, and the female judge ordered him to remove his hands. Out went his hands and down went his pants, and the question of "boxers, briefs, or commando?" was answered. It was not a good day for me or my client.

And consider the flipside: I had a client who didn't have a lot of money, though he managed to pay me and buy a nice shirt and tie for court. We would go to court, and he would arrive on time and sit in the front row, always wearing the same dress shirt and tie. This went on for about five court appearances. He had two charges, and it was touch or go as to whether he would go to jail. The prosecutor was insisting on jail and before the last court date, I called him to take one more shot at straight probation.

"Is your client the guy who always wears the same shirt and tie and sits in the front row?" the prosecutor wanted to know. "That's him," I said, to which the prosecutor replied, "Okay, I'll agree to probation because he is one of the only defendants who shows any respect."

Dealing with clients is one thing—they're in a jam and usually accept that you're their only way out of it—but sooner or later, you will come across the bane of a lawyer's existence. This is an individual so repulsive, so loathsome, that he or she can make any criminal defense attorney's skin crawl. I am speaking, of course, of the Relative Who Knows Everything. It goes something like this. You are representing a young man who committed an armed robbery. He should be facing 20 years in jail, but through your skill and hard work, you've arranged an amazing deal: He'll only serve about nine months. It's the deal of the century, a deal so good it borders on an injustice. Then, suddenly, your client stops returning your phone calls, and you know something is up. The day before court you get a call from Uncle Bill. (You've never met Uncle Bill because when it came time to hire and pay you, Uncle Bill was conspicuously absent.) Uncle Bill accuses you of incompetence and of ripping the family off. Why should his nephew go to jail? It's his first offense! I respond, because Junior stuck a loaded gun in somebody's face and pulled the trigger, and when the gun—or "ratchet," as they say in the street—jammed, he substituted it for brass knuckles, that's why.

So, what exactly are Uncle Bill's legal qualifications? Is he a lawyer? Did he work in a law office? Perhaps he is a retired police officer? No, it turns out he honed his legal chops during a 12-year stint in Rahway State Prison.

"I was a paralegal in jail," Uncle Bill says, without the slightest hint of irony (or shame, for that matter) in his voice. Now, about the only thing Uncle Bill can lecture you on is how to make a shank out of a toothbrush or how to concoct prison napalm (mix bleach and shampoo and heat in a microwave) but here he is, opining that you suck as an attorney and that any boob could get his nephew a walk.

Despite the late nights, crazy clients, and Uncle Bills of the world, and while chances are you'll never become a millionaire, you can make a comfortable living working as a criminal defense attorney. Once you've built up your practice, you can expect to earn as much as a partner in a medium-sized local law firm. (As I always say, add $50,000 annually to your actual earnings because that's the benefit you get from working for yourself.) If you take your craft seriously, the work can be intellectually challenging, and you will certainly meet some interesting people. All in all, I really can't see myself doing anything else, and for a guy with no discernible talent (except for telling inane stories), I'm doing all right.

***

It was late afternoon, and I was in my office. I had no court obligations that evening, and I was ready to go home. I stopped by Robin's office to let her know I was leaving. She asked about my day, and I said I'd spent the entire morning before a particular Superior Court judge. Once she stopped laughing, she related the following story.

About 25 years earlier, this judge was a Municipal Court judge in Trenton, and in those days, actions for paternity were filed in that jurisdiction. Robin was representing a pregnant woman who had been sleeping with three brothers—call them Charlie, Jimmy, and Vinny—and had brought an action for paternity. All three men were tested and the likelihood of paternity came out as Charlie 34.2 percent, Jimmy 33.9 percent, and Vinny 32.9 percent. The judge ruled that Charlie was the father.

Robin's client was not happy with the decision, as she considered Jimmy the real catch of the group. She didn't want an Uncle Jimmy, she wanted a *Daddy* Jimmy. She filed a motion for reconsideration stating that the test numbers were within the margin of error. The judge denied it. She filed an appeal, which was denied at the Superior Court. Determined that justice be done, she went to the appellate court only to be denied again. After years of court appearances, Charlie was definitively declared the father.

Can you imagine Thanksgiving with this family?

"Bless us Oh Lord and these thy gifts which we are about to receive from thy bounty, through Christ our Lord. Amen."

"Vinny, pass the sweet potatoes please and Jimmy, you deadbeat dad, I'm going to kick your ass in court tomorrow, Be-atch!"

What is wrong with people?

7

THE JUNGLE

I had been working on Nate's case diligently but was making about as much progress as a hamster on a wheel. After two tries, I'd gotten his bail lowered to $10,000, and a long month after that, his family put together the $1,000 to bail him out. Three and a half years in jail and Nate finally hit the streets. Within two days, he had a job. There was no partying for Nate, no reason to be happy. His charge had not yet been resolved.

I had been trying without success to locate the woman who had been working the register next to the robbery victim, in the hope that she could help clear up the identification issue. Through my investigator, I learned she still lived in Trenton, and at one point I actually talked to her on the phone, but she didn't want to help. She was slipperier than an eel in a bucket of soapy water, refusing to give a formal statement and dodging our attempts to serve her with a subpoena.

You might be surprised to learn that women are often more difficult to track down than men. Derek the bail bondsman, who was known to do a little bounty hunting on the side, once told me that female prostitutes are the hardest to locate since they're used to working underground and frequently change their appearance. They easily blend into the shadows. Men are easy to find, mainly because most of them have only one thing on their mind. Just find out where the girlfriend lives, camp out, and sooner or later (usually sooner) the guy will show up for a "booty call."

A buddy of mine who worked Internal Affairs for the Department of Corrections (DOC) described how male inmates spend years preparing an escape; some of the breakout plans are positively ingenious, worthy of *The Shawshank Redemption*. When the big day comes, they implement their well-thought-out plan and make good their escape. What do they do next to ensure a clean getaway? Is a car waiting to whisk them off to Texas, where some coyotes smuggle them across the Rio Grande to begin a new life? Of course not. The first thing they do is high-tail it over to Livingston to see their old fling. Our budding John Dillinger is inevitably picked up within 24 hours, usually in his girlfriend's bed.

Every now and then there's an inmate who *wants* to go back to jail, and my friend at the DOC shared one such story. An inmate who had a short time left on his sentence was given permission to attend the funeral of a close relative who had died. A corrections officer drove him, and after the service, the two were invited to a family get-together. The corrections officer thought, why not? They went and had a whale of time—in fact, the corrections officer got bombed. Back at the jail, the lieutenant in charge was getting worried; the men were three hours late, and the officer had not called in. No sooner was an alert issued than the government car pulled up to the entrance gate. To the amazement of the guard on duty, the inmate was at the wheel with the corrections officer passed out in the back. No way was Mr. Short Time going to take a hit because some lightweight corrections officer couldn't hold his liquor!

In Nate's case, the unwillingness of the witness to testify was not surprising. There is the problem in the inner city of retaliation against those who cooperate with the police. As the saying goes, "snitches get stitches," and while retaliation against witnesses is not very common, it does occur. I had a public defender case where I was assigned to represent a real thug on some third degree offense; at most, he was facing one or two years in prison. The State had one witness to call, and she had made it clear she didn't want to testify. The prosecutor kept pushing, and not long before the trial was set to begin, the witness was found dead—shot in the head while sitting in her car, presumably waiting for somebody. Was she set up? Nobody knows for certain, but the indictment against my client was dismissed, and I've been bothered by this case ever since. When the same client got into trouble again, he called to ask me to represent him, this time privately. Needless to say, I passed.

Witness intimidation is not the sole province of the criminal set. I was once involved in a federal case where I had a very viable motion to suppress evidence based upon the fact that the motor vehicle stop was illegal. The police had written in their report that they'd pulled my client over in Trenton for banging a U-turn without signaling. One thing led to another, and they found a gun in the car. I filed a motion, and the judge set a scheduling order. The government wrote the first brief and relied upon the facts in the police report. The Assistant U.S. Attorney obviously had insufficient knowledge of New Jersey motor vehicle law, because as I pointed out in my brief, you can legally make a U-turn without signaling as long as it doesn't affect other traffic. After submitting my brief, I received a response brief from the Assistant U.S. Attorney stating that somehow the police report had left out the "minor" detail that my client had pulled in front of another vehicle prior to making the U-turn, and thus his failure to signal gave the officers the probable cause for the stop.

This was complete, absolute bullshit, and I had a witness to prove it. A local businessman had seen everything. In fact, he had told my client to move his car, thus leading to the encounter with the police.

The other car was a fabrication, created by the government once they realized they might lose. Complicating matters for me was that my initially cooperative witness clammed up and then dodged my subpoenas. When my investigator finally got hold of him, the witness said he "didn't see nothing." I found out later that he was reluctant to testify against a Trenton policeman, fearing the cops would retaliate by stopping and hassling his customers, citing them for the most minor infractions. They had done it to others, and there was no reason to think they wouldn't do it to him.

I do almost no federal practice, and that's my preference because once the Feds take a case, there is very little you can do for your client. When the M1 tank known as the Federal Government comes bearing down on a defendant, you're not even a speed bump in the road. Do you think the judge will intervene? Hell, no! A federal judge is about as useful as Vin Diesel's comb when it comes to upholding the Constitution for people charged with criminal offenses. The judge will inevitably rely upon the precedent set in the case *Dirty Harry v. The City of San Francisco*, which stands for the legal proposition that "I am all broken up about that man's rights." If you are some flag-burning freak or think terrorists have more rights than U.S. Marines, then you have a friend in the Federal Judiciary. If on the other hand, you are an American citizen charged with a crime, well, the Bill of Rights sure as hell doesn't apply to *you*.

If you think I'm exaggerating, consider the following. I recently read an article panning the Mexican Criminal Justice System. Mexico doesn't have juries; defendants are tried before a panel of three judges, and the burden is on the defendant to prove his innocence. The author of the article believes this system to be unjust (and probably corrupt), and to support his position, he points out that Mexican prosecutors have an 80 percent conviction rate. While this may sound high, consider the fact that in United States Federal Court the conviction rate is over 90 percent! In other words, if you are charged with a crime, you have a better shot at a fair trial in Guadalajara than in the Southern District of New York.

During the U-turn and weapons case I was defending, the Assistant U.S. Attorney and I found ourselves sitting in a large, ornate, and empty courtroom on a Wednesday morning waiting for a chance to conference the matter with the federal judge. At precisely 11:00 AM, we were ushered into the judge's chambers, which were almost as large as the courtroom and equally ornate. The impression I had was of an Israelite being led into the "Holy of Holies" in King Solomon's Temple. The judge greeted us and led us over to a couch, some interview chairs, and a coffee table. She asked the U.S. Attorney to sit in a chair on her right and motioned for me to take the couch.

As I took my seat, I suddenly realized I had been ensnared by the La Brea Tar Pit of couches. Like a doomed saber tooth, I sank into its depths, my butt almost touching the floor and my knees at my chin. For the next 10 minutes, I was ignored in my growing discomfort as the two comrades in arms merrily discussed their college experiences, life at the U.S. Attorney's Office, recent vacations, fashion, weather, and even my case. Eventually the judge remembered I was there and, with an air of ennui, inquired, "What do *you* think?" (She had forgotten my name at this point.) My lung capacity was reduced perhaps by 80 percent due to the man-made trap that had engulfed me, but I managed to croak out, "Your Honor, there is no need for testimony. I stipulate to the police report."

Immediately, the atmosphere in chambers changed, and there was a moment of stone cold silence. I felt like an earthworm as the judge glared down upon me from on high, regarding me as a 14th-century

English duchess might a wretched serf begging a loaf of bread to feed his starving, plague-ridden family. Then, slowly and distinctly, she declared with utter contempt in her voice, "We … don't … do … that … up … here."

I thought she was about to shout "Release the hounds!" but Her Honor went back to chatting with my opponent, She of the Magically Appearing SUV. After another five minutes, the judge brought the meeting to a close. The Assistant U.S. Attorney bounded out of her chair glowing at the great time she'd had bonding with a federal judge. I somehow managed to extract myself from the remorseless maw of the defense attorney–devouring sofa and limped out of the sanctuary with a nasty backache. Needless to say, my head was handed to me during the motion to suppress.

To return to Nate's case, I thought the cashier's unwillingness to testify was extreme as well as misguided. After all, she would be testifying on this person's behalf, not against him. And this was a Lawrence Township Police investigation rather than Trenton PD. In addition, during our one telephone conversation, I had explained that my client was 50 years old, with no record, and that her own description of the assailant did not jibe.

One thing I've learned in my work is not to expect too much from people. By taking that approach, instead of being disappointed on a regular basis, I am pleasantly surprised when someone rises to the occasion. It's just like politics—well, outside of the "rising to the occasion" part. As the old political joke goes, the mayor is standing on a street corner conversing with a friend when a local walks by and gives him a dirty look. The mayor turns to his friend and says, "I don't know why he's so mad. I never did anything for him."

I tried everything I could think of to get the State to dismiss the charges against Nate. I used the old Hartmann charm, but even that didn't work. I appealed to the prosecutor's sense of fairness. That fell on deaf ears. I threatened to file motions. That had even less impact than the charm offensive. I begged, "Come on now, where's the love?" No dice. I *did* get the State to agree to consider a counter-offer of a plea to a disorderly person's offense. I set up an appointment for Nate to come to my office. When he arrived, I invited him to sit down at the conference table so I could go over the case with him one more time. I advised him of the State's new offer, thinking his recent taste of freedom might have altered his hard line on innocence. Who was I kidding? Not a thing had changed. If anything he'd become even more recalcitrant since his release. This client wasn't pleading guilty to *anything*. The only outcome he'd accept was a dismissal, and that dismissal had better come with a big fat apology. Yeah, like *that* was going to happen.

I have found in my years of practicing criminal law there are three types of indictable cases (matters indicted by the Grand Jury and resolved in Superior Court). The first type is the "first time offender" case, which usually involves a first (or even second) time offender who picks up a fourth or third degree charge. The defendant is not facing the possibility of jail, though this is not to say the charge isn't serious. Even without a jail term, a criminal conviction has far-reaching ramifications. It can cost a person his job and make it much more difficult to find future employment. It can result in deportation if the defendant is not a U.S. citizen, and in this situation, the lawyer must do everything in his power to keep his client from acquiring a criminal record. Merely keeping him out of jail is not a win. Short of getting the case dismissed, you must either get the client enrolled into a diversionary program known as pre-trial intervention (PTI) or convince the prosecutor to reduce the charge to a disorderly person's offense, thus avoiding an upper court conviction and a criminal record. Remember that because the prosecutor knows a conviction will not result in incarceration, he will typically be amenable to a plea agreement favorable to the defendant.

A good negotiating technique I learned along the way should be mentioned here. If there's a case you're close to working out but you're not quite there, try to wait the State out until June, when the judicial year ends. In June, the judge is thinking about how to make his numbers look as good as possible for the AOC and will put pressure on the prosecutor to resolve cases before July 1. The judge may also try to put pressure on you, but again it is your job, with all due respect, not to give a shit what the judge wants if it is bad for your client. Just remember the ancient adage, "When June comes around, the offers go down," and you'll be fine.

The second type of indictable case concerns "the pest." Pests are clients who smoke way too much weed and continually pick up little charges. I have represented a number of pests, and I've found that they are generally pleasant and even funny people to be around. They just keep doing stupid things. Initially, this type of client will have a whole bunch of marijuana charges and perhaps a few shoplifting cases in municipal court. He will then do some harder drugs or receive stolen property or throw a brick through a storefront window at 1:00 AM in order to break into a business—nothing *too* serious, but he is on his way and ends up on county probation. It continues this way for a couple of years; your client might have six municipal court convictions and be on probation for three Superior Court matters. He's like a soldier running back and forth across enemy lines, a drink in one hand and a joint in the other, bullets flying and shells bursting around him, somehow remaining relatively unscathed.

Then, one day it happens. The pest runs straight into a machine gun nest and with one quick burst from the gun's smoking barrel he is laid low, vanquished, cut down on the field of battle. Usually, he's caught dealing drugs or committing a second degree robbery, and he lands in jail. Because he has so many charges there is little you can do besides get him a flat three and have the violations of probation run concurrent. The pest is gone for a year, maybe a year and a half. Then one day he reappears ... bowed, perhaps, but unbroken.

The third type of indictable case is where the client is facing a serious charge that will result in jail time if convicted, sometimes substantial jail time. These are the cases where all bets are off. They're also the cases where a lawyer makes his reputation and earns his money. Any lawyer can be successful working the first two types of cases, but it takes a good lawyer to be consistently successful with this third type.

There are a number of books on trial advocacy, most of them written by or about famous lawyers such as Clarence Darrow or F. Lee Bailey. These books present a litany of successes where the author cites how the famous attorney—more demigod than lawyer—snatches brilliant victories out of the jaws of defeat. While these books entertain, they are of little value as practical learning guides. They remind you of what you won't become; for instance, in F. Lee Bailey's autobiography, we learn that Mr. Bailey traveled in a Learjet, while most street attorneys can only strive to afford a pre-owned Mercedes before they turn 50.

If you want a good practical guide on how to practice criminal law successfully, I suggest you start with Alistair Horne's *The Price of Glory*—a book on the history of the battle of Verdun. Verdun was an epic struggle between the Germans and the French during WWI. Fought in 1916, it was the bloodiest and ghastliest battle of the

Great War. Horne relates how German storm troopers and French *poilus* shot, machine gunned, gassed, and shelled each other into oblivion for months, clawing and killing over small corners of mutilated and blood-soaked Alsatian earth, as both sides expended tens of thousands of young troops over places like Fort Vaux, Le Mort Homme, Côte 304, and Fort Douaumont. This book is a must-read for budding lawyers.

When you have a serious case, and it is you and your client *contra mundum*—when everyone, including your wife, thinks you are a menace to society for representing such a creep, or when the State is trying to put your client away for a long, long time—then you must be like Commandant Sylvain Eugène Raynal and hold Fort Vaux at all costs. It is time to lock and load, because you are going into battle. You must be willing to bring the spade down on your opponent's head and split his skull—within all ethical guidelines and with due courtesy, of course. That's your job, and your client expects and deserves nothing less.

Most people have the impression that the most important part of a case is the trial. While trials are obviously very important, what occurs pre-trial is just as important and in some cases more so.

Some of the best advice Roger Daley ever gave me was the day he said, "John, the prosecutor will never give you a good deal unless he knows you can hurt him at trial." What exactly does that mean? It took me a while to figure out, but just as one can gradually find wisdom and enlightenment in a passage from Confucius, I've come to understand it thusly.

In every serious case in which you are involved, your attitude from the get-go has to be that you are "taking it to the hoop." From day one, you need to prepare your case like you are going to put 14 jurors in the box. You must be willing to aggressively investigate a case and to have an aggressive motion practice. By following this formula, I have had more success with cases before trial than at trial. In fact, most cases can be worked out through pleas, but in order to get the right plea offer, you have to show the prosecutor you are willing to go to trial and, through your investigation and motion practice, you must position yourself to win. In other words, you need the prosecutor to believe you could hurt him at trial.

Like everyone else, I closely followed the O. J. Simpson murder trial on television. I recall one of the commentators who was pro-prosecution bemoaning the fact the defense was spending more money on its investigation than the State. If this was the case, and I don't know if it was, then it was probably the first criminal case *ever* where the defense had greater resources than the State. Think about it: The State can rely upon the police and detectives from the municipality to investigate the crime. If the local police can't handle the job, every prosecutor's office has a small army of investigators working for it. In addition, you have the state police labs doing the forensic work. Prosecutors like to stack the deck and the small army of law enforcement officers they have backing them up gives them a tremendous upper hand in every case.

It is imperative to have a crack investigator working for you. In fact, in many cases, it's more important to have a good investigator than a good lawyer on your side. Over the years, I have had two excellent investigators work for me, Ross Bowen (now retired) and Mike Taylor. Both men are ex–law enforcement. Ross was a detective for the New Jersey State Police, and Mike worked as a detective for the Middlesex County prosecutor's office. The benefits of investigators being ex–law enforcement are threefold. First, they have the training. Second, they have the contacts. Third, they can pack heat. Ex–law enforcement have a license to carry a weapon, a huge advantage. I once sent Ross into a really shitty neighborhood in Trenton to track down a witness. Some members of the Bloods, who controlled this particular section of the capital city, started to harass him. He moved his jacket aside to reveal his Smith and Wesson. The situation rapidly improved. It was a perfect example of how to win friends and influence people.

Police investigations can be surprisingly sloppy, especially in high crime areas like Trenton. Detectives have to close cases and move files off their desks. Once they have a suspect, it isn't their responsibility to punch holes in their own case; they can leave that up to the defense attorney. Still, you might be shocked at the number of defense attorneys who don't use private detectives. The reason is simple: It costs money to hire a PI. Lawyers have enough problems getting paid themselves without expending additional money for an investigator. Unfortunately, it's an expense that must be borne.

There are always two sides to every story: The police give one side, and it's up to you to get your client's side. This can only be done by interviewing witnesses, and in every case where I have hired Ross or Mike, they've uncovered something that made our case a lot better. Is your client accused of stabbing someone during a bar room fight? Track down witnesses who will state that the alleged victim was highly intoxicated and picked up a bottle first. Was your client accused of hitting his girlfriend? Take a new statement from her; she probably doesn't want to proceed against her paramour because they are in love again. Has your client been indicted for eluding the police? Take statements from the three people he was working with, fixing up his house, when the supposed car chase occurred.

I have had clients who were facing life who were able to walk out of jail after one year because my investigators tracked down the right people and asked the right questions. Witnesses to an event rarely have exactly the same story. It is your job to find a weakness in the State's case and exploit it to your client's advantage. An offer involving state prison may just go to straight probation if the prosecutor feels you could win the case at trial because of what your investigation uncovered. I can't overstate this fact: *A good investigator will help even out the tremendous advantage that the State enjoys in all criminal cases.*

In addition to employing a private investigator, a criminal defense attorney has to be willing to aggressively file motions. If investigating a case is the offense, motion practice is the defense. If the matter was presented to the grand jury improperly, file a motion to dismiss the indictment. If there was a search, file a motion to suppress evidence. If there was a statement, file a motion to suppress same. If there was a photo lineup, file a motion to exclude any identification as being improperly suggestive. If a witness who helps your side of the case has disappeared, file a motion to have that person's statement read to the jury. If there was a confidential informant, file a motion to reveal his identity. Your attitude has to be that you are going to fight it out over every issue.

Motions are important for four reasons. First, you may actually win the motion. Second, where the motions involve testimony, especially in cases with photo lineups, you may be able to cross-examine witnesses outside of the presence of the jury, potentially gaining valuable information by asking questions you would not dare ask during a trial. Third, even if you lose the motion, you are creating issues for appeal. As I said earlier, many judges are loath to grant defense motions in criminal matters and would rather let the appellate division worry about it. So give the appellate division something to worry about. Finally, filing motions drives prosecutors crazy. Remember, prosecutors are state employees, and they don't get paid to work harder. Motions will almost always result in the plea offer going down, and a good motion can knock a couple of years off a person's sentence. Why? Because an afternoon of the prosecutor's time is worth a couple years of your client's. Is your client facing three years in state prison? Put pen to paper and that offer will go down to six months county time. If the offer is 10 years with a four year stip, file a motion to suppress with a brief pointing out the State's weaknesses and all of a sudden the offer goes down to a flat five. Even if your motion is only eight pages of suck, it will usually be worth something.

I have been doing motions for years, and I have saved almost all of them. In my computer, I have accumulated an evil brief bank from which I can summon forth the Furies of legal research at a moment's notice. As the Revolutionary War flag exclaimed, "Don't tread on me"; my personal tagline reads "or I will bury you under paper."

For the right case, with the right issues, and with a little luck, an over-the-top motion practice can be a thing of beauty. I was involved in one such case, when I represented a prostitute called Cookie against a charge of murder, where everything broke my way, and I can honestly say that an attorney has never represented a client more effectively.

I was assigned as a pool attorney to Cookie's case by the Mercer County public defender's office about a year after the murder had occurred. Her prior lawyer had fought with the public defender's office over billing and, in a huff, turned in all his pool files. Anyway, he probably didn't want anything to do with Cookie's case because it was a piece of crap. Once I reviewed the file, I realized that prior counsel was smart for unloading it. The outlook for Cookie was bleak.

A man in his fifties was found beaten to death in an area of Trenton known locally as "the Jungle." The Jungle was located a couple of blocks from the Trenton police station and consisted of two acres of abandoned and environmentally condemned wasteland, polluted by a long ago demolished factory that had poisoned the land with turn-of-the-20th-century toxic chemicals. The seething ground was overgrown with huge weeds that grew as high as a tall man and sickly swamp maples that barely grew higher than the weeds. It was an area traversed primarily by addicts and prostitutes. I remember reading a statement from a witness who frequented the Jungle, who told how at night she would hear cats screaming as they were attacked and devoured by giant possums that dwelt in the Jungle's depths. It was right out of the Apocalypse, real *Snake Pit* stuff.

The police's initial suspect was an individual known by his street name, "Half Dead," a man who had been committing robberies in and around the area for months. "Half Dead" was a particularly fitting name for this revenant, zombie-like creature who haunted the Jungle. I had actually met Half Dead once before, when his father, a decent, hardworking man, talked to me about representing his son. I visited Half Dead in jail, and I can assure you that his moniker aptly described him. He was my age but had been smoking crack and shooting heroin for close to 20 years. He was scary enough in jail; he must have been a terror at 3:00 AM in the Jungle, hunting in the brush for a victim so he could feed his habit.

As street names go, "Half Dead" was probably the best I ever heard, right up there with "Clean Head-J," "Apache," "Baku," and

"Sweet Pickles." The worst street name I ever came across belonged to a high-ranking member of the Bloods street gang. People called him "Pooh." I never did find out if he was named after excrement or A. A. Milne's lovable and cuddly bear who had an affinity for honey.

Anyway, the focus of the police investigation quickly shifted away from Half Dead when a witness came forward and claimed to have seen Cookie attack the victim in the light of a full moon. Apparently Cookie, the victim, and two individuals named Tre and Rosta had been smoking crack and drinking late one night in the Jungle. They smoked until there was only one small rock left, and then like four squirrels fighting over a nut, they fought over that last piece of crack. One of them ended up *dead* over that last miserable piece of rock. According to the witness, Cookie beat the man over the head with the eagle-shaped head of her cane and, once the victim was down, stabbed him in the eye with her eyeliner pencil.

Cookie gave a statement that she was at the beating but that Tre and Rosta did it. She accidently hit the victim in the head with her cane while coming to his defense, and when her eyeliner slipped out of her pocket the victim fell on top of it, impaling his own eye. She further stated that the dying man's final words were, "Thank you, Cookie." While not completely inculpatory, the story was so far-fetched that nobody would believe it. While this was in and of itself bad enough and would almost certainly convict her, the final blow was the forensic evidence. The victim was killed by blunt force trauma to the head. Recovered from Cookie's apartment was her eagle cane, with the beak broken off. It could easily have caused the fatal blows and corroborated the witness's story. Even more damning was the fact that in the victim's eye was a piece of black material that resembled—you guessed it—graphite from an eyeliner pencil. I had done enough trial work at this point to realize that the case was going to be a tough one.

After picking up and reviewing the file, I gave the prosecutor a call. I had read the offer in the file: Plead to aggravated manslaughter and the State would recommend 25 years. Given the facts, this was not an unreasonable amount of time but I wanted to know if there was any possible movement on that number. The prosecutor didn't want to negotiate against himself but he informed me that he would consider a counter offer of 20 years with cooperation against the co-defendants. Okay, I said, I will run it by my client.

I met Cookie that afternoon at the workhouse. The meeting did not go well. She had no idea who I was and, in fact, barely knew who her prior lawyer was, as she had not seen him for over six months. I introduced myself and went through my experience. I then went over the case, which, according to Cookie, was all lies. She maintained that she really liked the victim and had done nothing to him. I could tell right away that she had some psychological issues and was probably bipolar. But I didn't know how disturbed she was until I told her the plea offer of 25 years. (Apparently nobody had ever told her about the plea, even though it had been on the table for a couple of months.) When she heard the number her eyes bugged out of her head and she let out an unearthly, banshee-like shriek. I didn't have time to tell her that I could get her offer down to 20 years; she kept on shrieking and hyperventilating. The guard ran back and asked if everything was all right. I almost responded, "Hell no, everything is *not* all right," but I held it together and said, "We are fine." I finally calmed Cookie down by telling her that while it was my job to inform her of the offer, we weren't taking shit because she wasn't guilty.

As I was leaving the workhouse, I thought about my strategy. First, I had to get Cookie to trust me so I could convince her to take a deal if a good one came our way. This was no small order. She had been a drug addict and a prostitute for God knows how long, and there was no telling how she had been abused by people, especially men, over the years. Cookie didn't trust anyone; I would probably be the first since her childhood. Second, I would have to drag the case out for as long as possible. Drag it out and hope, if not for a miracle, for a big break, a really, really big break.

The first part of my strategy turned out to be easier than I expected. Every chance I could, I visited Cookie at the workhouse. If things were going on in her case, I visited Cookie. If we had court in a couple of days, I visited Cookie. If I was seeing other people at the jail and I had some extra time, I would visit Cookie. I found out we had one thing in common: We both had roots in Philadelphia and loved the Phillies and the Eagles. So we would talk sports. It took a couple of years, but eventually our conversations would go something like this:

"Man, Cookie, Donovan McNabb really sucks. Did you see him Sunday?"

"Hartmann, you don't know what the fuck you are talking about, and no, I didn't see him on Sunday. I was in the hole for fighting."

"Cookie, you are fucking crazy. Have you ever seen McNabb march down the field with less than two minutes on the clock and score a game ending touchdown? And why the hell were you fighting? I told you no fighting!"

"Hartmann, you a good lawyer, but you don't know shit about football. He takes us to the playoffs every year. And I was fighting because some bitch wouldn't shut the fuck up."

"I'm tired of the playoffs. I want a Super Bowl and a parade down Broad Street. And you've got to ignore other people talking trash."

"That ain't McNabb's fault, that's Andy Reid's fault. He sucks and I'm not gonna let some bitch mouth off 'CAUSE YOU KNOW MY KNUCKLE GAME IS ALL THAT."

"I agree with you on that, Andy Reid does suck, and throw it down as much as you want; you never listen to me anyway."

And so the preparation for our murder case progressed.

As for the delay in the case, that partially took care of itself. Nobody in the prosecutor's office wanted to deal with this case, so they passed it around like, well, like a football. The initial prosecutor did some work, but when September came and he was assigned to another division, he got out of it. A new prosecutor took over, saw the three crazy co-defendants, and dumped it after six months. The judge knew the trial would eat up months of his schedule and was more than happy to oblige my dilatory ways. Finally, after two years, the case was picked up by a new prosecutor who knew what he was doing and didn't mind grinding it out. The case also made its way to a new judge.

At this point, my motion practice kicked in. I filed the basic motions such as a motion to dismiss the indictment and a Miranda motion. But what I did next was really creative. The one witness who claimed to have seen Cookie strike the victim had her own baggage—she was a drug addict and a prostitute with a prior conviction for giving false testimony. She also had some psychological issues. I filed a motion for her medical records. Eventually, the motion was granted. This caused the prosecutor all sorts of problems because she was in jail in Connecticut for arson and her medical records were there, but he eventually provided the records. Based upon the documents I received, I filed a motion to have the witness evaluated by my expert. (Once doctors get involved in a trial, there is no end to the potential delay.) To my great surprise, the motion was granted. The witness was finally transported to New Jersey and examined both by my expert and another provided by the State. By this time, we were more than three and one half years into the case.

We had our other standard motions, which we lost, but through which I obtained some excellent fodder for trial. Eventually, a trial date was set, nearly four years after the event.

And then came Cookie's really big break. No one from the prosecutor's office had bothered to test her cane for blood or to test the particle in the victim's eye to show it was graphite. They assumed they had the case in the bag. However, with the fight I was putting up, the new prosecutor realized he needed the forensic evidence for the *coup de grâce*. The tests came back from the New Jersey State Police Lab and, lo and behold, the results knocked everyone on their ass. There was *no blood* on Cookie's cane and the particle removed from the victim's eye was not from an eyeliner pencil, it was vegetative. Maybe we were lucky, but as Ty Cobb said, "I make my own luck." Either way, we suddenly had a chance of winning.

Jury selection started around June 30, right before the July 4th weekend. Because of my client's statement, Cookie was being tried alone; her co-defendants would have to wait for their own day in court. Finding jurors for a murder case is difficult enough, but for this case, with the holiday around the corner, it was next to impossible. We spent all day trying to pick qualifying jurors, but after eight hours and one hundred prospective jurors, we had only eight people who could serve, and this was before I or the prosecutor had wielded any of our challenges.

At the end of the day, the judge called us into chambers and started to talk deal. The prosecutor was resistant, and Cookie had told me she wasn't pleading. But the judge kept on pushing and told everyone to keep an open mind.

Unbeknownst to me, after court that day, the prosecutor attempted a Hail Mary pass. He had always viewed Cookie as the heavy so he reached out to the other counsels to cut a deal. For three years, I had been fighting the case tooth and nail. Co-counsels never joined in on the motions and really took the attitude of "let's wait and see what happens to Cookie," assuming she would be convicted and they could get good deals after the fact. As a result, they had built up zero rapport with their clients. The prosecutor talked to one lawyer but could not reach the other. After not seeing his attorney for months, one of the co-defendants received a visit from his lawyer and was told he had to testify against Cookie that week in exchange for a deal. Not surprisingly, he said no. It was too last minute.

The next morning the prosecutor could see he was beaten. His case was falling apart. The judge wanted the trial to go away. We couldn't pick a jury. Resigning to fate, the prosecutor offered us five years. Cookie would be done with her sentence in three months. I went to the holding cell where Cookie was waiting for me and told her the news. Initially, she was resistant to the deal. But all that time I had spent with her over the previous years had paid off. She trusted me. We filled out the paperwork and went before the judge, and I talked her through the factual foundation. She pled guilty and got five years. From 25 years to basically a time-served sentence. I earned my money on that case.

I never heard from Cookie after sentencing. I hope she is doing all right.

8

THE DEVIL'S LEFT HAND

According to Waylon Jennings, "A pistol is the devil's right hand." Well, if a pistol is the devil's right hand, a crack pipe is his left.

During my first year practicing law in Middlesex County, I represented a very young man accused of selling drugs. For whatever reason, I felt compelled to take him to the side one day before court and talk to him about leaving behind his life of crime. He seemed to be listening to me, so I asked him, "When you're selling drugs"—I didn't have the lingo down yet; the proper way to say it would have been "when you're hustling"—"how much do you make in a night?"

"One stack," he responded.

"What's a stack?" I inquired.

"One thousand dollars" was his answer.

"Holy shit! You make a thousand bucks a night?" I exclaimed, shooting him a surprised look.

"Yes, sir, I do. Might even be able to make a little more on weekends," he matter-of-factly replied.

I am thinking to myself at this point that, like a schmuck, I'm hustling this kid's file for the State, making $22.50 an hour, and he's bringing in a thousand dollars a night, tax free. And it wasn't like this guy was the Big Homie for the local chapter of the Cripps; he was just some low-level dealer slinging drugs on the corner of Easton and Suydam Streets. I ended that conversation quickly, saying, "You know what, don't listen to me," and after that day, with only one or two exceptions, I stopped giving clients advice on how they should lead their lives.

There are occupational hazards to dealing. At my client's next court date, he looked distressed. I asked if anything was wrong, and he told me the police had found his friend's body over the weekend, in an abandoned house, tied to a chair with a bullet in the head. His friend was 17 years old. I told my client I was sorry. He just sadly responded with resignation in his voice, "Streets got all wins, no losses."

Easily one half to two thirds of all street crime is committed because of drugs, either directly through the sale and purchase of controlled dangerous substances (CDS) or indirectly by people committing crimes to acquire money to fuel their habit. America has been fighting a war on drugs for almost 50 years, though if you throw alcohol in the mix, we've been fighting a war on addictive substances for well over 200 years—all the way back to the Shays' and Whiskey Rebellions, both fought over the taxation of moonshine. In this war, America has had its butt kicked in a big way. Everyone knows there is a problem; what is the solution?

A couple of years ago, I was having a discussion with a client at the Mercer County holding jail. The jail was a creepy old building situated behind the criminal courts. It had once been a fully functioning jail but was now used solely to house defendants who were brought down for the day from the workhouse to go to court. Lawyers who wished to talk with their clients would have to walk in through a sally port and check in with a guard. You would then be buzzed through a ponderous wrought iron gate that must have been at least 50 years old and weighed two thousand pounds dead weight. Next, you'd catch a creaky, slow-moving elevator to the third floor where the inmates were held. Other parts of the building were abandoned, as I discovered when I once accidently hit the second floor button. The door opened, and I walked out. I realized my mistake but it was too late; the elevator had already closed and had slowly begun to meander to another floor. I hit the "up" button and waited alone in the dim light. It was evident to me that the room was the old dining hall. From a dark corner I could have sworn I heard a faint clanking and the low, indistinguishable mumbling of a long ago conversation. The conversation ended, and there was complete silence except for the groaning of the ancient elevator. By the time the elevator door opened, I couldn't wait to get out of there and on to my business. Perhaps it was my imagination, but from then on, I always thought if a place *could* be haunted it was that eerie old building. It has since been torn down and replaced by a temporary structure, and I can only guess that the ghosts of the prisoners who died there have moved on.

Getting back to the conversation with my client, here was a young man charged with the murder of a rival drug dealer. Due to some holes in the State's case (holes I created, by the way), the prosecutor assigned to the case was offering him 10 years in jail. With the time he had already served and other considerations, he would do another six years behind bars—a pretty light sentence for laying a man in his grave. On this morning, we were talking about the deal he'd been offered, and after some discussion, he decided to take it. We filled out the four-page plea papers and then, with the work done, we had a brief opportunity just to talk about things in general. Not in a judgmental way, but really in the spirit of small talk, I asked him why he dealt drugs. He explained that he had no high school diploma and that finding a job in the inner city was very difficult, especially when you had a criminal record. By the middle of the month, the public assistance was all used up, and his infant son would need formula and the rest of his family would also need help. So he sold drugs to support his family. The conversation was an eye opener for me. This guy was hustling not so he could have that big car or expensive clothes but to keep his kid from going hungry.

About an hour after this conversation, I had my eyes opened again. Before we could put the plea through, the prosecutor and I had to run the deal by the judge. We told her the deal was for 10 years, and she responded in so many words that while the time was a little light, she was okay with it because it was "just another drug dealer" who'd been killed. Now, I'm no bleeding heart liberal by any means, and I love the *Death Wish* movies as much as any redneck, but when the judge said this I thought, "Wow, that's a little harsh."

I represent a lot of drug dealers. Most of them are small time, dealing either bags, decks (10 bags), or bricks (50 bags) of cocaine or heroin. Marijuana is also very popular, and pills are prevalent among suburban white kids. Crack has really fallen out of favor. It's primarily used by the hardcore older addicts, like an old client of mine who was caught passed out in the driver's seat of a Dodge Durango sitting in the middle of a busy county road. He had eight thousand dollars cash on him along with three and a half ounces of crack. To smoke the crack, he was using a run-of-the-mill glass pipe, but instead of a regular lighter he had a blow torch. That, my friend, is a man on a mission. That, my friend, is hardcore. He was going to end his day either cuffed to a bench in a police station or in a coffin.

Methamphetamine, usually referred to as "meth" or "crystal meth," is virtually nonexistent in Mercer County, mainly because it is almost impossible to set up a meth lab in a densely populated area and avoid detection. However, it is a major problem right across the Delaware River in Pennsylvania. Marijuana, on the other hand, is the "safest" drug to sell. I was once having a conversation with a narcotics detective from the New Jersey Criminal Justice Department. I asked him, theoretically, if he wanted to sell drugs, what would he sell and how would he go about it. Without missing a beat, he said he would move marijuana in quantities of less than five pounds. As long as you keep it under five pounds and your jacket is clean, you will not go to jail when you are eventually popped.

I should mention that when it comes to marijuana, refer to it as "weed" and not as "pot." The latter is antiquated and your client will picture you with a mullet haircut (party in the back, business in the front) in high school in the '80s. However, if you are talking with a Jamaican client, you'll want to refer to "weed" as "tea" in order to show that you are up (or is it down?) with the lingo.

Selling drugs is a business, and it can be extremely profitable—maybe not quite as profitable as being a Goldman Sachs investment banker, but then there are some things even a drug dealer won't stoop to. One duo of dealers I knew was grossing tens of thousands of dollars a week selling cocaine. While this might seem unlikely, the math was pretty simple. They would drive up to New York City to Broadway and 141st Street (this is not the actual street) and would pick up one or two kilos of cocaine from their Dominican contact. (According to them, the Dominicans are by far the best group to deal with—they provide the purest cocaine, are businesslike, and will only rarely rob or kill you.) One kilo of cocaine cost them $17,000. Once they brought it back to Mercer, cut it with baking powder or whatever else was available, and bagged it, they could sell a gram for up to $90 to the right people. Their $17,000 investment could turn into $90,000, minus normal wear and tear (that is, what the two used to party).

As with any other commodity, the price of cocaine varies over time. I have heard that the supply of cocaine is restricted during a presidential election year and the price goes up. The reason for this is unclear.

Another drug with high profit margins is oxycodone pills, known as "oxies." People can buy them, often legally, for a few dollars a pill and then resell an 80 (as in 80 milligrams; they also come in 30s and 40s) for $60 or more. The worst drug to sell is heroin. The client base is located primarily in inner-city Trenton; the people who buy it don't have a lot of disposable income, and the competition is fierce among dealers and the gangs with whom they are affiliated.

As far as the gangs go, in Trenton the Cripps have a small presence and the Latin Kings are also around, but the Bloods dominate. The Bloods are not a unified group; in Trenton they are comprised of several sects including the Sex Money Murder sect and the Gangsta Killer Bloods, otherwise known as G Shine, otherwise known as GKB. Not satisfied with the Blood hegemony over New Jersey's capital city, Sex Money Murder and Gangsta Killer Bloods focus on fighting each other. A few years ago, there was an all-out war between the two gangs resulting in more than 20 murders in one year. The situation was completely out of control, and the police began a major crackdown where they basically threw the Fourth Amendment out the window and started stopping, searching, and arresting every suspected drug dealer they could find. Things have gotten a little better recently, and the murder rate is way down; the drug dealers are off the street and selling from homes. But the competition is still stiff, and you often hear of a bag of heroin being

sold for as little as $5, whereas 10 years ago they were being hus-
tled for $20 (or even $25 to college kids) and you better not have
been a dollar short when you showed up. Now, at $5 a bag, make
certain the product is not "beat," because if it's car battery acid and
you shoot it up, you're dead.

For drug dealers, one of the biggest problems is how to hide all
the cash they accumulate. An individual I represented told me that
he kept $100,000 hidden in an air duct in his basement. He got into
a fight with his old lady, and she hit him with a restraining order,
forcing him out of the house. His wife didn't know about the money,
but he couldn't get back in for it. Eventually, he called the police
and had them escort him to his residence. Once inside, he went
down into his basement and loaded up a duffle bag with his cash.
Under the watchful gaze of two police officers, he walked out of the
house with all his ill-gotten gains, never to return.

Not everyone is cut out for the business of dealing drugs. The
most inept drug dealer I have ever seen was a young man who
decided he was going to live the gangsta lifestyle. He set up shop in
a roadside motel in Carteret and started hustling. Unfortunately for
him, his only clients were three undercover cops. No joke, he sold
exclusively to the police. The cops kept on buying and he kept on
selling, oblivious that they were running up the score. Even with
about 20 sales, all of them caught on tape, I might have been able to
keep him out of jail. Unfortunately, he made a big mistake. One day,
a detective knocked at the door, and he was lying on the bed, too
lazy to get up. He told his 17-year-old brother to go to the door and
serve the detective. All of a sudden, he was facing a second degree
offense for employing a juvenile to sell drugs. He wound up doing
a flat five.

Because drug dealers are businessmen of sorts, they make some of the best clients. Hiring an attorney is part of the cost of doing business, so they usually have the ability to pay. By and large, they show up for meetings and make it to court on time, and when it comes to getting a deal, they do not have unrealistic expectations. They are pretty good at taking your advice. Almost all dealers get caught eventually. When they do, they can either get a lucky break because the police made a mistake during the search; they can plead guilty, often with jail time; or they can cooperate with the police as confidential informants against other area dealers in order to "work off" their time.

The way a drug dealer works off time is as follows. Say the abandoned row house that your client is using as a stash house is raided while your client is in it. The police find a handgun and 60 bags of dope. Because your client has a prior charge for distribution of CDS, and because there is a weapon, and because the house is within one thousand feet of a school, he is facing a lot of jail time. Technically, he could do 20 years, but in reality he is facing somewhere in the area of 12 years with a four-year stip. You review the case, and the search warrant is solid. The only way to avoid jail, which your client is eager to do, is to cooperate with the State. You arrange a meeting at the courthouse, usually on a Friday around 3:00 PM because nobody is around. You then go with your client to the basement and meet with a detective and an assistant prosecutor.

A side note: Things are more difficult if your client is not on the street but incarcerated; in that case, the client has to be brought down from the workhouse as if he were going to court. The detectives will never actually go to the workhouse to meet with people, saying it is too conspicuous. Personally, I just think they don't want to be bothered to take the drive. On the way to his fake court appearance, your client is whisked away by a sheriff's officer and brought to the interview room. You just hope nobody saw them and that the sheriff's officers won't say anything.

At the meeting, you are provided a letter from the prosecutor stating that whatever your client says at the meeting cannot be used directly against him; this is sometimes referred to as a "Queen for a Day" letter. Your client then tells the detective and prosecutor all the shit that he's been up to, who is selling what to whom and how they are moving it and where they are storing it. It is obvious throughout these meetings that the detectives know almost everything that is going on in the streets. After listening to your client, they decide if they want to work with him and, if they do, they bring out a contract to sign. The contract is basic stuff, stating that the client can only work under the direction of the police but is not an agent of the police, and that if he is caught doing anything illegal, all bets are off. It also gives the amount of time each job will reduce your client's sentence. Now, it used to be that a defendant would have to do maybe one or two jobs to reduce his sentence to probation, but not anymore. A few years back the Attorney General set new guidelines for how much an individual gets for a particular job, and the new numbers make Ebenezer Scrooge look like Old King Cole.

A defendant who works a first degree job gets two years off the front number and one year off the back. A defendant who does a second degree job gets a one year reduction from the front number and a measly six months off the back. The same crappy numbers that apply to a second degree offense apply to a third degree offense. For a fourth degree job, the hapless defendant gets a pat on the back and a kick in the butt.

These numbers border on violating the Thirteenth Amendment (that's the one outlawing slavery), but as Richard Nixon's notorious aide Charles Colson was purported to have said, "Once you have them by the balls, their hearts and minds will follow." What makes it worse is that if you're doing a job and you bust an entire gang and 20 people are arrested with first degree charges, you only get credit for one first degree case. Twenty people may be going to jail, but you are only getting a stinking two-year deduction. To get a job done, a defendant has to do at least two and sometimes three controlled buys before the police have enough information to apply for a search warrant. To work off 10 years, you basically have to become an indentured servant to the State.

If drug dealers make decent clients, drug users tend to make lousy ones. They don't have a lot of money because they spent it all on drugs, so you are usually hired by family. Because they are *still* on drugs, these clients rarely show up on time, often miss meetings or, even worse, miss court. They are terrible at taking advice. Just try talking sense to some shaky, nervous wreck sitting in your office who is more cranked out than Axl Rose after he's banged a speedball and drunk a gallon of Red Bull. To say the meeting won't be productive is an understatement. And don't forget that for a drug dealer, everything is a business—they are not going to take unnecessary risks or commit pointless crimes. It is the wide-eyed drug addict jonesin' for heroin who commits the residential burglary or cracks grandma over the head in order to grab her pocketbook. They call addicts "fiends" for a reason.

I truly believe, after observing the problem firsthand for more than 15 years, that the reason illegal drugs are such a plague on our society is that while selling them is illegal (which I believe it should be), possessing them is, for all intents and purposes, semi-legal. Dealing drugs brings with it the risk of a very real and severe penalty, and our jails are full of drug dealers. Unfortunately, when one dealer is arrested, another is there to take his place, whether on a street corner or as a larger supplier. Dealers are willing to take the risk because a lot of money can be made and there is never a shortage of demand. On the other hand, while possession of heroin or cocaine technically carries a penalty of three to five years in jail, I do not recall anyone actually going to state prison for merely possessing CDS.

Possession of CDS is the only crime you can commit time after time, year after year, and not go to jail. If a user is caught with a couple of bags, the case is usually downgraded to municipal court because prosecutors don't want to deal with it. If the matter goes to Superior Court, then the defendant invariably gets straight probation. Typically, the most severe penalty a user will face is probation with the condition that they pay some fines and complete a long-term in-patient drug program. I won't go so far as to say that drug rehab programs never work, but from my experience, they are not very effective. Many people can change on their own; they just don't really want to.

This might sound a bit insensitive, but people who get hooked on drugs by and large treat their addiction as a crutch. A show about addiction on the Discovery Channel looked at an experiment in which a group of monkeys were given access to morphine. I forget how the monkeys medicated themselves, but they could take as much as they wanted by pressing a button attached to the distributor. Monkeys apparently have a pretty strict social system, and the lead monkey in this experiment wouldn't touch the stuff. He was king of the hill and apparently didn't need drugs because he was already high on life. The further you went down the social ladder, the more likely a monkey was to use the morphine. On the bottom rung was a poor little male monkey. The other male monkeys were beating the crap out of him, and he was getting no love from the ladies. His life sucked. He was pounding the primate happy button every five minutes.

I think it's pretty much the same with people who use drugs; life sucks so they start using. However, the psychosis of drug addiction goes deeper than that. Now they have become the center of attention. "Oh, so and so is using heroin, he needs help." We fawn over him in court, trying to get him into a program. Parents, guilt-stricken thinking they are responsible for their adult child's problems, spend all their time worrying about this wayward kid. And as to all the bad and irresponsible things that the addict has done— stealing from his parents, his lack of responsibility, the disappointment and embarrassment he's caused—all is forgiven because of his "disease." Well, the way I see it is that shooting up heroin is not a disease, it's a crime, and maybe we should start treating it like one.

Since the beginning of America's war on drugs, all of the focus has been on supply, with almost none on demand. Perhaps we should stop treating users as victims and start treating them like criminals. The first time you are convicted, you go into a diversionary program. The second time you are convicted, you are placed on probation. The third time you are convicted, you do a year at the county. The fourth time you are convicted, you go to state prison for four years. Harsh? Maybe, but it would result in demand going down, drastically.

America's dependence on illegal drugs has wrought tremendous grief all over the world. Think of Colombia in the 1980s and early 1990s, and how many tens of thousands of people died there because of the cocaine trade. Think of the terrible situation in Mexico, where there is a bloody and vicious civil war raging over supplying drugs to the U.S. And think of the poppy fields in Afghanistan, exploited by the Taliban to finance their war against us.

It appears that the current general trend is toward decriminalization and legalizing drugs rather than the other way around. Imagine—50 years from now, most drugs will probably be legal and the only hustling will be done by IRS agents. After all, drugs are a major business, and the government wants in on the action. The dealer on the corner will be replaced by the U.S. government, selling prescriptions for heroin, cocaine, and crack as a cure for anxiety and headaches. Uncle Sam will be the Big Homie and Dr. Feel Good wrapped into one. Then again, having the government handle drug distribution might not be a bad idea: The resulting high prices and inefficiency could bring the drug trade to a screeching halt within five years. After all, who the hell wants to deal with a government bureaucrat while they're strung out on heroin? Imagine this scenario:

Addict: "Hey man, I need a bag of smack, bad."

Bureaucrat: "Fill out this form, the L-23, and take it to Window 17 to get stamped; then bring your stamped L-23 back to this window."

Addict: "Oh man, I just waited an hour in this line. Come on, man, just give me a hit, I'm really hurting here!"

Bureaucrat: "Once we approve your stamped L-23, the waiting time to pick up your bag of smack will be approximately 10 days. It will come in a plastic bag with "Do Not Forget to Recycle" stamped on it. Call 1-800-Gov-Drug with your order number to find out when your smack is ready. Pick-up is at Window 40. Now, I am required to ask if you are registered to vote and to offer you a voter registration form if you are not."

Addict: "Huh? What sort of place is this? I'm writing my Congressman, man!"

Bureaucrat: "Sir, you may write to whomever you want. In the meantime, it will be $200 for the bag of smack. Pay at Window 8 and then present the receipt to the teller at Window 33."

Addict: "*What*? I ain't got no $200, man, just $15 in crumpled-up singles!"

Bureaucrat: "In that case, fill out this form 404b and take it to Window 31. The Mexican Drug Cartel offers a financial assistance program for indigent junkies."

American bureaucracy—it's enough to set anyone straight.

9

TOOLS OF THE TRADE

No doubt about it, trial work measures the mettle of an attorney. And yet, amazingly, most lawyers do not try cases. In fact, the lawyers considered to be the most successful have rarely sat at counsel table during a jury trial. Not one of our current U.S. Supreme Court Justices was known for his or her prowess before a jury. Indeed, I don't know if any actually ever picked a jury, even though I like to believe that they must have. The attorneys you find in those high-priced Manhattan law firms specialize in transactional work and rarely if ever see the inside of a courtroom. And, of course, they're laughing all the way to the bank. But I would argue that there is nothing more rewarding for a trial attorney than to hear the words "not guilty" emanate from a jury foreman's mouth. (Okay, a $100,000 bonus probably comes close.)

A successful defense attorney once told me that the reason he went into criminal law is because it is the one area of the law where an individual attorney's skill has a huge impact on a case. Nowhere is the impact of one attorney more important than during a trial. By picking the right jury, asking the right questions, and arguing the proper points, a lawyer can change the outcome of a trial.

Americans are obsessed with team sports. It seems like we all grew up playing T-ball, Little League baseball, soccer, football, and basketball, just to name a few. Before we even put on a helmet or grabbed a bat, we were exhorted to "be a team player" or to "win one for the team." But let me tell you something, as someone who went through the system, who played team sports (though not very well) from Little League up to college, I can now say with confidence, "Screw the team." So-called team sports are really just a way for average schmucks to do all the work, so that one person—such as the quarterback or pitcher—can get all the glory. Team sports are suburban serfdom, where you give it your all, put in 110 percent, make every sacrifice necessary, just so some other guy (usually the biggest asshole on the team) can impress the girls. Rugged individualism, the trait that forged America—that made the likes of Daniel Boone put on his coonskin cap, grab his flintlock, and head over the Appalachians because things were getting "too crowded" in 1780s Western Pennsylvania—has been laid low by the mindless collectivism cultivated on the municipal soccer field. Is it gone forever?

No, I say. Rugged individualism is still alive and well in trial work. In trial work, it is *all* about the individual. It is all about *you*. You are *it*, the thin red line, the beginning and the end, the Alpha and the Omega. If you mess up, it's *your* fault, and you can't blame the offensive tackle who let a lineman through for the sack. And if you win? Well, dump that big container of Gatorade all over your own head, because you did it yourself. To misquote my Little League coach, Mr. Nelson (who happened to be a great guy), there is no "team" in "I" when you are trying a case.

On the Nathaniel Smith case, the prosecutor, Nate, and I had been going around in circles for about six months. The entire negotiating process deteriorated to my begging the State to dismiss the charges. Unfortunately, all of the prosecutor's witnesses were still in the area and willing to testify again. Nobody would just let the damn thing go. The alleged victim, the cashier at Halo Farms, wouldn't let it go. The detective wouldn't let it go. And Nate sure as hell wasn't letting it go.

I have to hand it to Nate for being a man of principle. People love to talk about their principles, but let's face it, how many men (or women) of principle do we really know? During the short time I was involved in politics, I never met anyone I'd call a true man of principle. In the practice of law, with the possible exception of Roger Daley, I never said to myself after meeting someone, "Wow, that guy really sticks to his principles."

Perhaps I'm a little cynical, but it seems as though everyone has his price. My father is a scientist, and he used to say that you could leave 10 crisp one-hundred-dollar bills on your lab table for a week and nobody would touch it. A hundred scientists would walk by and not one would think about sticking the cash into his lab coat pocket. However, if you were to leave a novel idea, a Nobel Prize–winning kind of idea, scribbled on a piece of paper on the same lab table, that scrap of paper would be gone in no time flat, nabbed by some sticky-fingered PhD. If you think that's an overstatement, just look at Watson and Crick, who won the Nobel Prize for the elucidation of the structure of DNA. They stole some of the concept from another scientist, a woman with whom they worked. I know of this sorry scientific saga through a documentary I saw on public television. And if it's on PBS it must be true.

Nate was facing jail, again, and he could make the whole thing go away by saying one little six-letter, two-syllable word: "Guilty." But he wouldn't utter the word, he wouldn't even think about the word. It wasn't part of his lexicon; it wasn't part of his being. What would you do in that situation? Would you be that unmovable mighty rock, impervious to wind, water, and time? Or would you be the weed growing on a railroad track, trembling at the faintest vibration emanating from the approaching freight train? Personally, I am leaning toward weed.

Nate loved the Bible, and quotes from "The Word" flew off his tongue like he was filled with the Holy Spirit. When I think of Nate, I think of what Jesus said in Luke, 6:47–48, "Anyone who comes to me and listens to my words and obeys them—I will show you what he is like. He is like a man who, in building his house, dug deep and laid the foundation on rock. The river flooded over and hit that house but could not shake it, because it was well built."

Nate's faith was in the Lord, and that was where it was going to stay. On a Monday morning in January, I was outside the courtroom with him, filling out the four-page trial memo and going over the penalties if convicted (fortunately, he could not receive more than his original sentence of seven years if convicted again). Our final conversation concerning the plea offer of straight probation in return for a guilty plea to "Theft from the Person" went as follows:

"Nate, I am going over the plea with you one last time. I am not trying to have you take it because I know you won't, but I have to go over it with you so we can assure the judge that you've been given the offer. So, will you plead guilty in exchange for a sentence of probation?"

"No, Mr. Hartmann. I trust in the Lord and I won't plead guilty. I am innocent."

"Okay, the answer is no."

I checked off the answer as to "What is the final plea offer?" on the trial memo and reviewed the remaining questions with my client. At this point, I couldn't help thinking of a joke I'd heard in church a number of years back. There was a terrible storm with massive flooding, and a town had to be evacuated. One man decided to stay in his house. A boat came by, and the ship's captain called out to the man, "You have to come with us, there is flooding and you will soon be inundated." The man responded, "No, I will stay here, my faith is in the Lord." The flooding continued and a few hours later, the man was forced to the second floor of his house. Again the boat came by and the captain yelled, "You must come with us or you will certainly drown." Resolutely, the man responded, "No, my God has never abandoned me, I will remain!" The boat went off. Three hours passed, and the waters kept rising. The man was now on his roof. The rescue boat came by one last time, and the captain shouted, "The levee has burst; you will drown in 10 minutes if you don't come with us." From the pinnacle of the house, in the howling wind, a determined voice sang out, "The Lord is my Salvation, I will not leave!"

Ten minutes later the man is standing at the Pearly Gates, face to face with God. The recently deceased says, "Lord, I don't understand. I have served you my entire life, I have worshipped you, and I have obeyed you. Why did you abandon me?" God replies, "Well, I did send the boat three times."

As I signed the trial memo with Nate that January morning, I hoped we weren't missing the boat.

Nate's trial was scheduled for May, so I had plenty of time to prepare. During his first trial he had not testified, and when I asked him about this, he said his lawyer had advised him against it. The prosecutor who had conducted the State's case during the first trial was widely considered to be one of the very best trial attorneys in the office, and Nate's first attorney said it would be best not to go up against him. This time around it would be different; I was going to stick Nate on the stand. The prosecutor who had originally secured the conviction was no longer on the case; in fact he was no longer at the prosecutor's office. The new prosecutor we would be going against was relatively young and inexperienced. We could handle her just fine, I thought, and I believed Nate *had* to tell his story because it made sense. If you tell the truth, stick to the facts, and keep your cool, you will do fine on cross-examination. (Conversely, if you are going to lie your ass off, go off on tangents, and blow up at the slightest provocation, then you'd better assert your Fifth Amendment right to shut up.) All that's needed is careful preparation, which means having your client come to your office at least three times and putting him through his testimony and potential cross-examination.

So, starting in March, I had Nate come to my office on a regular basis to work on his testimony. He had a halting delivery and spoke in what I could only describe as a 19th-century voice, reminding me of a character from history, though I couldn't quite put my finger on whom. Finally, one day, as we sat in my office going through his testimony, it struck me: Nate reminded me of the Northern Avenger—the great abolitionist John Brown. He was tall like John Brown. He spoke as I imagined John Brown would have, in a low, slow, but intense drawl. No jolly swagman was he; Nate was intense, and you knew that, just like John Brown, once he made up his mind, nothing on earth could move him to change it. That night I told my wife I thought I was defending "John Brown reincarnate." She smiled and gave me that look that only a loving wife can give a husband that said, "You're crazy, but you're *my* crazy," and then said, "Don't work so hard. You'll get him off. He's innocent."

By the eve of trial, I felt I had worked out the kinks in Nate's testimony. When my client hit that stand, he would be a testifying machine. He had his narrative down pat and was ready for any cross-examination that might come his way. "Yes, Mr. Prosecutor, my lawyer did tell me what to say—he told me to tell the truth." Nate was going to hit it out of the park. We were ready to roll.

I cannot stress this point too strongly: Never stick your witness on the stand until you've adequately prepared him. I've heard horror stories of what can happen if a defense witness is inadequately prepared. Case in point: In a murder trial in Chicago a couple of years ago, the defense attorney called his client, the defendant, to the stand. The first question the lawyer asked him was whether or not he had murdered the victim. The defendant cleared his throat, leaned forward, and declared, "I do not recall."

In one of my first trials, I was assigned to defend a New Brunswick drug dealer known as "Bigg Keon." Apparently, one of Bigg's clients—a young white kid—was delinquent in paying, so the dealer pulled a gun on him and took his money by force. The kid complained to the police, and Bigg was arrested. Given his extensive record, he was facing a mandatory minimum jail sentence of 25 years, but was much more likely to get 50 if convicted. My client remained in jail the entire time from his arrest until trial, and every time I visited him in jail and every time we went to court, he was adamant that he was not guilty. He wanted a trial in spite of the solid evidence against him.

This case hinged upon the testimony of the victim—the young drug user—and it became apparent as things progressed that the victim did not wish to testify. He wouldn't speak to my investigator, and he wouldn't talk to the prosecutor's investigator. Not that he wasn't around town—he was; he just didn't want to testify, and a person doesn't have to talk to the police if he chooses not to.

As a quick aside, if you have teenage children and the police ring your doorbell one day and ask permission to speak to Junior because he might have gotten into a little trouble, don't be Mr. Good Citizen and invite the cops in and instruct Junior to tell "Officer Friendly" everything. Instead, be Mr. *Smart* Citizen and tell the police that Junior has nothing to say, and then call a lawyer. You have no idea the number of times I have had parents in my office who tell me they thought they could trust the police but now their child is in the youth detention house and they are shelling out money to hire me.

Anyway, the prosecutor in Bigg's trial got so fed up that he called the victim and told him the State was subpoenaing him to testify and he'd better come to court or else he would be arrested. This rash statement turned out to be a big mistake.

The trial date came and things progressed fairly well for our case. I picked a good jury, gave a good opening, and when the investigating police testified, I scored some points. Finally, the State called their "star witness." It was showtime. I had prepared a pretty good cross-examination for him, as his original description of the perpetrator did not exactly match Bigg, plus the robbery was at night and the kid was high so I felt confident and ready to pounce. The witness was sworn in and took the stand. The prosecutor started asking him preliminary questions about what he was doing that night and how he happened to get stuck up. Then the prosecutor inquired, "Do you see the man who robbed you in this room?"

Now, keep in mind that Bigg Keon was the only African American in the entire courtroom at this time. The jury was all white. The judge was white. The staff was white. The prosecutor was white. The sheriff's officers were all white. And, in case you haven't figured it out yet, I am white. At this point, I expected the young man to do what every State witness does in cases where I represent a black client: Look over at the defense table and state that the perpetrator is the African American sitting next to the man in the suit with glasses. Not this time. The witness looked around the court, taking his time, and finally said, "No, I don't see him."

The prosecutor, his face suddenly ashen, said, "Take another careful look around and tell the jury if you can identify the man who robbed you at gunpoint."

Clearly enjoying his role as official wise guy and relishing the prosecutor's discomfort, the witness looked carefully at the judge, then looked carefully at a sheriff's officer, and then carefully examined all fourteen jurors one by one. He didn't look at the defense table. After a minute, he said, "No, he is not here."

The prosecutor walked over to the defense table and stood right behind my client (I should have objected, but I was inexperienced), shot his witness a scowling look, and said, "One last time, and I remind you that you are under oath, do you see the man who robbed you?"

"No, I don't," came the answer.

Aware that his case was going down the toilet, the prosecutor threw a Hail Mary and asked one final question: "Did anyone threaten you before you came here today?"

With a venomous glare the witness raised his right arm, pointed at the prosecutor and shouted, "Yes, *you* threatened me. You said if I didn't testify, you would put me in jail!"

There was silence in the courtroom before the judge finally cleared her throat and said to me, "Mr. Hartmann, do you have any questions for the witness?"

Putting aside my carefully typed-out cross, I said, "No, Your Honor. No questions." My client was home with his family a few hours later.

Soon after I'd passed the bar, I asked several attorneys how many trials it took to reach a high level of competence, and the consensus seemed to be about 10. To date I have done approximately 50 jury trials—not too shabby, but hardly an overwhelming number. There

are many attorneys out there who have done well over a hundred trials, and a few who have done two hundred or more. My general
feeling is that you need five trials under your belt to start getting
comfortable. It's like riding a bike, in that you can read all the
books you like about bike riding, but until you hop on that two-
wheeler and start pumping away, you can't ride. So it is with trial
work: You have to get before a jury and start pumping away to gain
any competence. That said, here are some pointers I wish someone
had shared with me when I got started.

First, when it comes to the tools of the trade, you won't need many.
There are three invaluable books you should always have handy at
counsel table. The first is Leonard Arnold's two-volume burgundy-
covered *Criminal Practice and Procedure*. Arnold was a prosecutor
and then a judge in Somerset County, in the heart of New Jersey horse
country. (Yes, that's right, New Jersey has a lot of horses and horse
farms, and while Jersey horses might not be the fastest, they are the
toughest and a Jersey horse can mud-stomp any Kentucky horse's hind
quarters anytime, anywhere; it's the Jersey way.) Somerset has one of
the highest per capita incomes of any county in the U.S. It also has the
biggest pain-in-the-ass prosecutor's office in New Jersey, one that
treats every file like the Lindbergh Baby case. Over the entrance to the
Somerset County Courthouse is some phrase in Latin. I don't read
Latin so I don't know what it says, but if I had to guess, it would be
something like, "He who enters here, abandon all hope." I know one
attorney who charges clients extra for cases out of Somerset, calling it
"combat pay."

Arnold, the author of the aforementioned *Criminal Practice*, had
a reputation as a tough prosecutor and as a curmudgeon on the
bench. I never appeared before him but I spent some time working
in Somerset Family Court, Juvenile Part, when he was sitting in

Criminal Part, and I got the impression from other attorneys that an appointment to appear before him would keep you tossing and turning in bed until the wee hours the night before. Curmudgeon or not, the man knew everything about criminal law, and reading *Arnold's* (which is what everyone calls it) will give you a firm foundation for criminal work, especially trials. Ninety-five percent of all the questions you will ever have are addressed somewhere within the covers of *Arnold's*. The Chinese Communists have Mao's "Little Red Book," and New Jersey defense attorneys have Arnold's "Medium-Size Burgundy Book."

Arnold's explains how to subpoena a witness from out of State and how to compel a witness to testify. The book spells out in detail how to find a theme for your case, how to give an opening (with some very helpful hints), how to deal with expert witnesses, how to cross-examine witnesses, what to say during summation, and what to ask for in a jury charge. It even has a chapter called "Successful Defenses." You have got to love that. *Arnold's* gives you all that you need to know and hands it to you on a silver platter. The book is invaluable. Just the other day I cited *Arnold's* to the court to support my position. The prosecutor actually had the balls to get up and say, "Your Honor, *Arnold's* is just a book."

Just a book? Is the Taj Mahal, then, just a mausoleum? Is Beethoven's 9th just a tune? Was Waterloo just a skirmish? Was Babe Ruth just a batter? Was Marilyn Monroe just a pinup? Were the Beastie Boys just three dudes from Brooklyn? What was this guy *talking about*? Had this been 1590s Westphalia, the authorities would have been tying him to a stake and firing up the kindling for such sacrilege.

My copy of *Arnold's* looks like it has been through the washing machine five times. Its cover has faded to pink. It is battered. It is bruised. It has yellow stickies protruding from about half its pages. Its pages are marred by lines of highlights and multiple marginalia. It is falling apart. It is beautiful.

Two other books I found to be extremely useful when I started practicing law are *Title 2C, New Jersey Code of Criminal Justice Annotated*, with comments and annotations by John M. Cannel, and *New Jersey Rules of Evidence*, by Richard J. Biunno. Both books provide excellent notes under each section and neatly and succinctly summarize the case law. More than once, Biunno has come in handy for me at trial when a prosecutor threw out some bullshit objection that had no basis under the law. Let the jury take their mid-morning break while I look up the truth in Biunno. Within 15 minutes, I'll set the record straight and have the prosecutor crying, running home to mama.

The final book I'd recommend is the catchily titled *Medicolegal Investigation of Death: Guidelines for the Application of Pathology to Crime Investigation*, by Werner U. Spitz and Russell S. Fisher. While not as broadly applicable as the other titles I've mentioned, Spitz and Fisher is a must-read if you plan to try homicide cases.

Lord Protector Oliver Cromwell would have loved Spitz and Fisher's book. When the butcher invaded Ireland in 1649, he quickly became known for his indiscriminate murder of Irish priests and peasants. His was the infamous order to Irish Catholics: "To Hell or to Connaught," which is the equivalent of telling somebody today to go "To Hell or to Mogadishu." While raging through Western Ireland, Cromwell came across a barren land called the Burren. Instead of admiring the Burren for its stark natural beauty, Cromwell bitched to one of his generals, "There isn't a tree to hang a man, there isn't a lake to drown a man, and there isn't earth to bury a man." Sweet guy, that Cromwell.

You have no idea how many ways there are for a person to die until you've read *Medicolegal Investigation of Death*. The first section of the book is on the "Identification of Human Remains," and it only gets more interesting after that. There is a section on trauma and disease followed by blunt force injury, followed in turn by sharp force injury. Then there is injury by gunfire, followed by thermal injuries, followed by asphyxia, followed by drowning. There are also sections on investigating deaths in childhood and deaths from drug abuse and alcoholism. I once had a murder trial where the State argued the cause of death was blunt force injury. I argued that improperly performed CPR caused the victim's death. Spitz and Fisher was invaluable for my research and my cross-examination of the medical examiner. The worst part about the book is that each section includes numerous photos of individuals who died from a wide range of ghastly injuries. For me, these disturbing images always bring to mind what Jesus said in Matthew, 25:13: "Watch out, then, because you do not know the day or the hour."

So, you have your client and you have your books. Now you're ready for trial. The first thing you do is pick a jury. The longer I try cases, the more I realize that picking the right jury may be the most important part of your case. Pick the right jury with the right frame of mind, and you dramatically increase your chances for a not guilty verdict. Pick the wrong jury, and you are going down.

The difficult thing about picking a jury is that you know almost nothing about these people. Just before the jury pool shuffles into the courtroom, you are handed a list of all the prospective jurors. The list provides each individual's name, town of residence, and occupation. Once everyone is seated, the judge enters and gives some preliminary instructions. As he is giving his speech about how the jury system is essential to our form of government and how jury service is the bulwark against tyranny, 50 percent of the potential jurors are thinking about how to get out of it. A small minority may find the speech inspiring, but most don't care. Hell, many of them don't even vote. What do they care about Henry II, Runnymede, or, for that matter, the Revolutionary War and the Bill of Rights? They could be home, mowing their lawns.

One judge I appeared before regularly, now retired, used to tell prospective jurors that any of them who didn't want to serve could leave, right then and there. They would appear startled, then even a little disappointed that they wouldn't be able to give their self-important, lame excuse, to explain why they would just love to serve on a jury but couldn't do it this week. Then, about half of the potential "citizens true" would get up and slink out the door. According to the judge, his feeling was that people who wanted to get out of serving would, so why waste everyone's time? This reasoning made a lot of sense to me.

One time, when Judge Markashevsky was picking a jury, a creepy-looking guy asked her for a side bar. He was the type of person who rubbed everyone the wrong way, with his long hair, bad tattoos, and worse attitude. He kept coming up with excuses as to why he couldn't serve, but the judge shot him down every time, just to bust his chops. With each subsequent denial, his eyes grew wilder and his excuses became more desperate: work—nope; children—find a relative; reasonable doubt—think about it; police—work with it. I was thoroughly enjoying his discomfort. Finally, he used the Nuclear Option: He said "I don't like black people." Judge Markashevsky looked at him with utter disdain and said, "You disgust me, you terrible man. You are excused." That was awesome.

Anyone can get out of jury duty simply by saying, "I just believe the police" or "I assume the defendant is guilty." The problem is that using such obvious ploys is like wearing a bathing suit at the beach for the first time during the summer: You can't possibly look good doing it. The key to getting out of jury duty is doing it with *style*, so that when you're leaving the courtroom, with your ticket to a free afternoon and some cold beers, people think to themselves, "There goes a real *mensch!*" So, here's how to get off jury duty and look good at the same time.

If you are a man, wear a jacket and tie. If you are a woman, dress like you're on your way to Sunday services. Almost everyone who appears for jury duty is dressed like a slob. If you are among the mass of humanity known as a jury pool in a suit and tie, certainly the defense attorney and perhaps the prosecutor will think to themselves, "This guy is way too serious, what's his angle?" During the questioning of potential jurors, or *voir dire*, say you would love to serve, that the job or the family vacation will just have to wait because justice beckons. Make a point of saying that as a U.S. citizen, you would consider it an honor to be on the jury. Insist that you can be perfectly fair to both the State and the defendant. This malarkey will fuel the defense attorney's paranoia because nobody talks like that. You'll be out of there with the first challenge. And as you walk out the courtroom door with all those admiring eyes upon you, keep your head held high because you, my friend, have turned the walk of shame into a triumphant exit. Know in your heart that since the founding of the Republic, generations of Americans have come up with every excuse under the sun to get out of jury duty, but nobody has done it with more class than you. You are a giant among a nation of shirkers. You are a Great American.

If you feel as though you can't pull this off, here's a one-liner for the prosecution. When the judge asks you if there is any reason why you cannot serve on a jury, simply take a deep breath and in a torn voice say, "Your Honor, I don't feel that I can judge anyone." If the judge doesn't excuse you, the prosecutor will knock you off.

In the late 1990s, when I'd started to take trial work seriously, I attended a seminar given by some nationally renowned trial experts. In their presentation on jury selection, I'd expected to hear about the type of people you want to pick, and when I say "type," I mean race, sex, religion, age—that sort of thing. Well, I was in for a rude awakening. The only advice these "experts" gave was to "pick someone who was accused of a crime and eventually exonerated." Oh really? Pick someone who was once falsely accused? What great insight. Thank you *so* much for that pearl of wisdom, that gem from Numbers, that message from on high. Pick somebody who was falsely accused. You guys must have really rubbed your brain cells together to come up with that one. Well, no shit, Sherlock. Everybody knows that—especially the State! Nobody who has been falsely accused of a crime will ever, and I mean *ever*, see the inside of a jury room unless the prosecutor is 90 years old and ready to take his seat at the drool table.

For years, I searched in vain for a guide on jury demographics that could be of practical use to defense attorneys. There isn't one, so, finally, I've written it myself.

Harvard Law Review, eat your heart out.

Hartmann's Politically Incorrect
Guide to Jury Selection

Picking a jury is like counting cards. It doesn't assure you of a winning hand, but if done properly, it increases the odds that you will have the best hand. When a prospective juror is sitting in the box, you know almost nothing about him. In New Jersey, the judge asks him basic questions: Is he married, how many children does he have, what type of work does he do, what does his spouse do, is he more or less likely to believe a police officer over other witnesses, can he follow rules laid down by the judge, etc. The court then might ask other questions, and you can also submit your own, such as, what do you watch on TV, what do you listen to on the radio, do you belong to any organizations, do you have any bumper stickers on your car, and so on.

You have to assume that people are lying during *voir dire*. Hell, I would! Do you think I'm going to tell a roomful of strangers that I watch *The Real Housewives of New York City* on Bravo with my wife on Thursday nights (my wife makes me do it, I swear) or that I never miss *The Soup* on E! on Friday nights? No way. I'm saying my favorite show is *Nova* on PBS, and I read *The Economist* religiously. I wouldn't want anyone to get the wrong idea about me.

The problem in jury selection, of course, is that you cannot look into a person's soul. But you can look at their face, and here's how you can increase your odds of getting a jury that will listen to you, take the presumption of innocence seriously, follow the judge's instructions, and maybe even return a not guilty verdict.

Before I continue, let me say that you may find my advice offensive in its reliance on racial stereotyping. Don't be an idiot. Do you want to sit around a campfire singing "Kumbayah," or do you want to get your client off?

You want blacks on your jury. You want Jews on your jury. You want liberals on your jury. These people are more likely than those in other groups to seriously apply the standard of proof in criminal matters, namely "beyond a reasonable doubt." Potential African American jurors in particular are to be coveted and protected at all costs. Prosecutors can excuse one African American, but after that you are entitled to what is called a *Gilmore* challenge, where the prosecutor has to put on the record the reasons he excused the second or subsequent African American. *Gilmore* challenges have to be done at side bar. However, when you make the challenge, say very loudly so that all the prospective jurors can hear you, "Your Honor, the prosecutor is trying to knock off all of the African American jurors." That will serve the prosecutor right for not playing by the rules.

You have to be wary of ethnic European types such as Germans, Italians, Irish, and Poles. We have come a long way as a nation, but people still have their prejudices, both overt and, more often, subconscious. A little trick I use to determine whether I want to consider keeping a person on a jury is to ask myself, "Would this man/woman mind if his/her daughter dated a black guy?" If the answer is yes, I will probably not be keeping this one on.

Hispanics, perhaps surprisingly, are hit and miss. As minorities, they may have friends or family members with immigration problems. On the other hand, they tend to be socially conservative and many have family in law enforcement. In picking a jury, one of my rules of thumb is that if I suspect a person may have voted for me when I ran for office, I won't let him anywhere near my jury. If I think he pulled the lever for my Democratic opponent, on the other hand, I want him in that box.

If I am going against a male prosecutor with a full head of hair, I'll try to pick at least one juror who is naturally bald, as I am myself follicly challenged. A bald guy is part of the team, and if the case is close, my brother will probably go my way. And, anyway, as Leviticus 13:40 tells us, "If a man's hair has fallen from his head, he is bald, but he is clean." It's good to have clean people on your jury.

I would stay away from Russian, Chinese, and Indian naturalized citizens (their adult children born in the U.S. are okay) because they grew up in authoritarian or patriarchal societies and may be predisposed to side with the State. As for Filipinos, I will never let one sit on my jury. Now, for all I know, Filipinos might be the fairest people on Earth. But I once had one on a jury—she was juror number five—and during my entire summation, she sat with arms crossed, giving me the stink eye, shaking her head in the negative every time I made a point as if she were the school principal listening to my lame excuse as to why I shot a spitball at my first grade teacher, Mrs. McGuire. I am not about to let that happen again.

An experienced attorney I once knew said he liked young people on his juries, the theory being that they are less likely to listen to authority. That said, watch out for young white males. I haven't had a lot of success with them.

When you pick a jury of 14 people (12 deliberating jurors and two alternates), you want at least eight women. Women will give you a better shot than men will. One of the best juries I ever had included 11 women. It was certainly the happiest jury I've experienced, and a happy jury is a good jury. They were always laughing and smiling. (Then again, what could be funnier than three stoners "hot boxing" in a car with four pounds of marijuana in the trunk who are pulled over because they almost rammed a police cruiser leaving a Taco Bell?)

If the prosecutor has a female victim, you want women jurors because women will judge her more critically than men will. If the prosecutor is an attractive female, you definitely don't want men on your jury. In one trial, I was going up against a young female prosecutor who was drop-dead gorgeous. The jury had nine men, and my client didn't stand a chance. The prosecutor was new and made all sorts of mistakes, but it didn't matter. During my opening, I noticed most of the male jurors were ignoring me and ogling my opponent. I looked over at her and saw that she was oblivious to everything except her nails, which she was carefully filing. My client was found guilty.

Having a lot of women on your jury will also increase the chances for a hung jury. As a female public defender once told me, "Two women can't agree on anything, how can eight?"

If a prospective juror mentions he knows somebody in law enforcement, knock him off. I don't care if he says the guy three houses down works as a janitor at the local State Police barracks, and they only see one another at Halloween. Get rid of him. And never let an engineer sit on your jury. Engineers are overly analytical and that is usually bad for your case. Otherwise, people with advanced degrees are desirable, especially liberal arts majors.

There will be times when you are tempted not to follow the principles of jury selection I've outlined here. You may be moved to risk it all and go for broke—to drive up to that proverbial fast food window, throw caution to the wind, and shout out "Super size me!" You might think to yourself that you should pick that nice older woman whose nephew is a police officer because she reminds you of Aunt Dolores. Don't do it! Knock that nice woman off the jury immediately because she is a guilty-verdict bomb that's sure to go off as soon as deliberations begin.

Your quest for the perfect jury is not unlike Sir Lancelot's search for the Holy Grail. So who, you ask, is the ideal juror and where can I find this person? She is a 50-year-old Jewish woman with a master's degree who reads the *New York Times*, watches *CSI*, and has a social worker for a daughter. You can't do any better. This Venus de Milo of jurors would give Charles Manson a fair shot if it weren't for the swastika tattoo on his forehead.

**

Of course, Hartmann's rules must flex according to the facts of your case. For instance, I had a case where my female client slashed another woman in the face with a razor blade and gave the victim a large scar, or, as they say in the streets, a "buck fifty" (that's 150 stitches). I didn't select *any* women for that jury. We beat the most serious charge and instead of doing five years in prison, my client did 90 days, all because of the right jury. An all-male jury, that is.

Now, I wouldn't want you to get the wrong impression. If there are 10 witnesses saying your client robbed the convenience store, and the security tape shows your client robbing the convenience store, and your client previously confessed to robbing the convenience store, *no* jury is going to find him innocent. However, most cases can go either way, and the outcome often hinges on subtle nuances. Increase your odds of getting a not guilty verdict.

Pick the right jury.

10

TEN GUILTY PEOPLE

It had rained heavily the night before the start of Nate's trial, but when morning broke the clouds were gone. The storm left in its wake a beautiful spring day. As I looked out my kitchen window a little after 6:00 AM, reflectively sipping my morning coffee, the sharp sunlight illuminated the vibrant green hues of the newly minted leaves. I opened a window and felt the refreshing touch of the cool, damp morning air against my unshaven face. About 10 feet from the window, a male wren was chirping in brief spurts of determined song, trying to attract a mate to his new home, a small pine bird house that I had haphazardly hung in an evergreen a few weeks before. Taking it all in, I had the sense that everything was going to be all right.

I finished a second mug of coffee, headed back upstairs, and showered. After shaving, I picked out my best gray suit and selected a blue shirt. When I was in law school, a trial attorney gave us a lecture on trial advocacy. He explained that he always wore a blue shirt at trial because a study had concluded that people were more likely to trust a person wearing blue. "Always wear big blue," he said. At the time, the advice sounded about as good to me as throwing salt over your left shoulder after dinner to keep the devil away, but whenever I am going to address a jury in either an opening or closing, I have on a button-down blue shirt. Next, I picked out a favorite tie, medium red with thin yellow and black stripes. I loved that tie because I saw the character Jack McCoy wear it on an episode of *Law and Order*. Finally, I dusted off my best pair of Allen Edmonds dress shoes. All in all, I was dressed very conservatively. In fact, I intentionally dressed the way a prosecutor should dress. No jury was going to mistake me for some typical defense attorney trying to pull the wool over their eyes. A jury was going to think, "Hey, he's wearing McCoy's tie. He must be telling the truth."

After a breakfast consisting of a toasted bagel with melted American cheese sprinkled with Tabasco sauce and washed down with V8 Juice, also jacked up with Tabasco, I brushed my teeth, kissed my wife and kids goodbye, got into my car, and headed to court.

In the back of my wagon was my black briefcase, not the brown one. The brown one is thin and expensive, and I've had it since 1991 when my parents bought it for me to celebrate my election to the State Assembly. The black one is fat, homely, and cheap. I bought it at Staples for 35 bucks. I call it the "sarcophagus," and on this morning, it was fully loaded. Inside its strained, thinly covered cardboard sides were my trial notebook, my file, a brand new legal pad, *Arnold's* (both volumes), rules of evidence, a statute book, my personal calendar, two pens, a highlighter, and my lunch bag that my wife had packed that morning. The thing weighed a ton, and if it weren't for the wheels on the bottom, I'd have been done for. In 1916 at the Battle of the Somme, English Tommies had to carry 60 pounds of equipment as they attacked, heading over the top and attempting to traverse two miles of machine gun–swept fields. (Ah … great plan there, General Haig.) Whenever I lugged my black box of legal dead weight up a flight of stairs, I felt a kinship with those soldiers, like I knew what they must have gone through—with the exception of my not being at the receiving end of a German Mauser.

Parking in Trenton can be a real pain, especially when the legislature is in session. If you want to park on the street, you have to

arrive early. I would have to park all day, and since the only free
street parking in the area is behind Sacred Heart Roman Catholic
Church and all the spots there are taken by 8:00 AM, I would be
parking in a pay lot. The State parking lot where I usually go is on
East State Street, about three blocks from the courthouse.

By the time I arrived at the court, it was a couple minutes before
9:00 AM. State court is not nearly as formal as federal court, and if
you are a few minutes late, it usually isn't a big deal with most
judges. The sheriff's officers waved me through the metal detector,
where I set off a brief buzz. I had been going to the courthouse for
years and nobody cared. Nate was waiting for me, standing in the
hall. He was dressed in his best clothes: a black suit, white shirt,
and black tie. On his feet were old worn dress shoes, the type that
might have paper in them to plug up the hole in the sole. We
greeted one other, and I told my client to wait there while I went
into the courtroom.

I walked into the courtroom and went up to the counsel table,
onto which I heaved the sarcophagus. It landed with a dull, heavy
thud. Already present in the courtroom were the court clerk and the
court reporter. The Mercer County Criminal Part has about five
court reporters working for the office. I have a love/hate relationship
with them. I know most of them fairly well, and, on a personal level,
we are all friendly. However, I have a tendency to talk quickly, and
there is nothing a court reporter hates more than a fast-talking
lawyer. And believe me, you want the court reporters to like you.
They can clean up your English and get rid of the "Ahs" and "Ums"
and "Okays" that pepper any accurate transcript, or they can put
everything down exactly as you say it and make the appellate judges
think the village idiot was conducting the cross-examination.

The court reporter looked at me and said, "Hi, John, remember the three-second rule." The three-second rule is that you are supposed to wait three seconds after a witness answers a question before you ask another. I responded, "Hi Roe, I won't forget." I was sincere when I made my promise to the reporter. At the beginning of every trial I swear to myself that I am going to speak slowly, but once cross gets going, it's going to be:

Witness: "I don't re—"

Me: "Whatdoyoumeanyoudon'trecallwhenyousaidtwominutes agoyouremembereverythingaboutthatnight?"

I unloaded the sarcophagus, then took a seat and waited. Shortly after 9:00, the prosecutor rolled in. She appeared a little frazzled, as though somebody back at the office had dropped a bomb on her five minutes earlier. She greeted me and started to put her files on the prosecutor's table, which was the table closest to the jury box. The clerk asked if we were ready to see the judge, and both of us responded in the affirmative. We exited the courtroom and walked the 10 feet to the judge's chambers, where we were met by a law clerk who ushered us in.

The judge was at her desk and asked us to sit down on the two government-issued chairs. She was familiar with the facts of the case, and the meeting didn't take long. We reviewed the anticipated length of the trial (only two days after jury selection) and reviewed any potentially unique issues (there were none). I then submitted to the court a few additional questions for jury selection. The prosecutor did not object, and the judge agreed to ask them. Once our discussion was over, the judge excused us, then called in a sheriff's officer and asked him to bring up the jury pool. I left her chambers and went out into the hall to get Nate.

Nate was sitting on one of the marble benches in the entrance when I approached him. I told him we were ready to proceed. He gathered himself slowly and stood up (Nate did everything slowly, he was perpetually deliberate). We walked into the courtroom, sat down together, and waited for the jury pool. At about 10:15, I heard the first shufflings of 100 feet outside the courtroom and the dull hum of multiple conversations. A few minutes later, one of the sheriff's officers said in a loud voice, "Jury entering." At this point, everyone rose from their seats. Everyone, that is, but me. I usually don't stand when a jury enters the room, and the reason is straightforward. Marty Matlaga, who is as I said the best trial attorney I know, doesn't stand, and if it's good enough for Marty, it's good enough for me. He has talked to jurors after verdicts and believes they are generally turned off by the obsequiousness of jack-in-the-box counsels. So when the jury enters, I usually remain seated; *always* in the case of jury pools. After all, half of them are just looking for some lame excuse to get off service—why the hell should I stand for them?

It ended up taking most of the day to select the jury. I had 20 challenges, and I tried to select the best jury possible. I also gave Nate wide latitude in who he wanted on the jury. If he was getting a bad vibe about somebody, I used one of my challenges. The prosecutor, on the other hand, used her challenges sparingly.

By the time we reached the mid-afternoon break, we had 14 in the box. I was very pleased with my handiwork. We had a number of African Americans as well as others whom I felt would be sympathetic to Nate's plight. There was even a professor from Princeton University sitting on the panel. A Mercer County prosecutor typically knocks off anyone affiliated with Princeton, whether they live in the town or work at the university, the theory being that they are

all *New York Times*–reading, Obama–voting, hybrid–driving, Cape
Cod–vacationing, United Nations–admiring, public radio–listening,
An Inconvenient Truth–watching, screaming liberals. I once
objected to the fact that Princetonians were being systematically
eradicated from the jury by the State. The judge, perfectly reason-
ably, asked me why Princetonians were a protected class of people.
I thought to myself for a second. They are wealthier than most.
They are more educated than most. They are predominantly white.
The best I could come up with was "geographical racism." The
judge said, "Good try, Mr. Hartmann" and allowed the prosecutor
to continue with his geographical cleansing.

The judge asked the prosecutor if she wanted to use a challenge.
For about the sixth time in a row, she stated, "No, Your Honor, the
jury is satisfactory." The judge then called my name. I looked carefully at the jury. I leaned over and told Nate that I thought the jury
was pretty good and asked if he wanted to go with them. Nate said
the jury was fine. I then rose and exclaimed, "Your Honor, this jury
is perfect." Nate's fate was now in their hands.

We had agreed that openings would wait until next morning. The
judge empanelled the jury, read them preliminary instructions, and
then sent them home. We were free to go.

Nate, the sarcophagus, and I left the courthouse a short time later.
We walked to the bottom of the steps and with a few parting words,
Nate went his way and I went mine. I had to go to court that
evening, for a driving while suspended ticket in Hamilton, but I had
a few hours to kill, so I went back to the office to catch up on some
work, put out a fire, review my opening statement, and prepare my
cross-examination.

The opening has to be strong. Tom Sullivan once told me about
a study claiming that half of all jurors have their minds made up on

guilt or innocence after the openings. Not after they've heard the testimony, not after the summations, but after the *openings*. It is that important, or scary, depending how you look at it. So, what do you say during your opening?

First, you need to have the right mindset. Whether you agreed with his politics or not, you have to agree that Lyndon Johnson was one of the greatest bullshitters ever to live. Long before throngs of Americans were chanting "L ... B ... J!" as Johnson bulldozed over Barry Goldwater in 1964 (by the way, Barry Goldwater actually won Princeton Township in 1964—what the hell has happened?), he had already acquired the nickname "Bull" Johnson as a freshman at Southwest Texas State Teachers College at San Marcos. When it came to being an advocate, Bull's advice was that you have to convince yourself that your position is the truth. Before you can convince others, you must convince yourself. And so it is in criminal trials: You need to convince yourself that your client really *is* innocent. Once you come to believe your own bullshit, you can sell it to a jury. If you can convince yourself of the righteousness of your cause, then at the opening you will come out all fired up and swinging. If you can't, then when you address the jury you will stick your hands in your pockets, mumble unintelligibly as you shift from foot to foot, and fail to make eye contact with the jurors. At that point, the trial just becomes one long sentencing.

Second, like most defense attorneys, during my opening I always focus on the standard of proof in criminal matters, which is "beyond a reasonable doubt"—the highest standard in the law. Let's face it: The criminal justice system is skewed to the prosecution in order to skewer the defendant. You are going against the State, and the State makes all the rules. The prosecution has all the money for the investigation, and judges are pro-prosecution. At trial, prosecutors are the first and last to address the jury, a tremendous advantage. (Not to mention that you are also hampered by the fact that your client is probably guilty.) The one card a defense attorney can play is "beyond a reasonable doubt," so you'd better play that wild deuce, and play it well.

Every so often you hear somebody talk about lessening the standard of proof in criminal matters, but it'll never happen. "Reasonable doubt" is the price we pay to give the false impression that everyone has a fair shot in court. So, start off your opening by mentioning reasonable doubt. Make certain you talk about reasonable doubt in the middle of your opening. And, finally, conclude your opening by reviewing reasonable doubt.

Third, focus on a few key points about the facts of the case and hit those. One strong fact may sway the jury, even just one juror, to find your client not guilty. If the witnesses said the perpetrator was over six feet but your client is five foot eight, mention that fact repeatedly. If the policeman saw the perpetrator for two seconds from 20 feet away and claims he can make an identification from that fleeting view, bring it up repeatedly. Go with your best pitches and stay in the strike zone.

Fourth, connect with the jury. When I just started doing trials, Jim Pfeiffer gave me some excellent advice. He told me that the key to having your client found not guilty was having jurors believe that they or a loved one could be sitting in the defendant's chair. Ideally, during your opening, you should be able to walk over to your client as he is sitting at the defense table, put both of your hands on his shoulder, and tell the jury, "Ladies and Gentlemen of the jury, you could be sitting right here." Of course, this is not always possible. If your client was caught with 65 grams of crack in his right pocket, a forty-five in his belt, and $2,156 in assorted bills in his left pocket, you can't say to the jury, "Ladies and Gentlemen, you, too, could have been caught with over one ounce of crack, while packing heat, with your winnings from the dice game the night before." But in cases that involve potential mistaken identity or self defense, try to have the jurors walk a mile in your client's shoes. If they do, you might just walk your client out the door after the verdict.

Fifth, unless your case is particularly complicated, keep your opening short. The ideal length is between 10–15 minutes. And don't pat yourself on the back while you're opening, thinking how brilliant you are as you go on and on. The jurors aren't sitting there because they are spellbound, they're sitting there because they are *jury* bound—they can't leave, or they would. Have you ever listened to a speech or sermon that lasted over 15 minutes and not thought to yourself, "When is this guy going to shut up?" (Hey, I'm willing to bet there were people sneaking down the hill 30 minutes into the Sermon on the Mount.) A jury can take it all in within 15 minutes; going on any longer will just try their patience, and it's a bad idea to start things off by convincing the jury you're a blowhard.

Finally, what do you do if your case really sucks? If the witness room is wall-to-wall with people just itching to point the finger at the miserable wretch sitting next to you? If one of those witnesses is a nun and your client confessed on video? What if the first time you practice your opening, you start laughing uncontrollably? What if the best opening you can think of is "Ladies and Gentlemen, do you like my tie? Do you think it goes with my suit?" What if you have a better chance of surviving Creutzfeldt-Jakob disease than getting a not guilty verdict? What do you do in such a hopeless case? A case where even St. Jude would say, "Sorry, buddy, can't help you with this one"? I'll tell you what you do. You attack. You attack once, you attack twice, and you keep on attacking. If you are going to die, do it with your boots on.

**

Nate's trial was scheduled to resume on Wednesday morning at 9:00 AM. I arrived at the courthouse at 8:30. Nate was already there, as usual, waiting for me. We went in together and sat down outside the courtroom. I took out the yellow legal pad on which I'd written the outline for my opening and went over it one last time. The opening was different from most of my other openings because Nate's case was so strong. I focused primarily on the facts of the case and put "reasonable doubt" on the back burner. I was making some finishing touches when I received a call on my cell from a vaguely familiar number. Against my better judgment I answered. The following conversation ensued:

"Hello?"

"Mr. Hartmann, it's Chris and—"

"Chris who?" I responded.

"You know, Chris from Middlesex," he answered in a panicked voice. "You represented me a couple of years ago." I still couldn't place him but didn't press the issue.

"Mr. Hartmann, I'm in Mississippi, and the police are trying to come into my house and are threatening to break down my door. What should I do?"

This question came out of left field and caught me off guard, but I tried to give Chris the best advice I could.

"Now, Chris, you say you're in Mississippi?"

"Yes, sir," he answered.

"And the cops are trying to break into your apartment?"

"No, they are trying to come into the house—they're banging on the front door. I'm upstairs."

"Are you certain they are police?"

"Positive."

"Well, Chris, I don't practice law in Mississippi. If this were New Jersey, I would suggest you tell them through the door that 'I'm not letting you in until I see a warrant,' but since you are in Mississippi, you better open the door. They don't play around down there— haven't you seen *Mississippi Burning*?"

Chris quickly responded, "Okay, thanks, Mr. Hartmann. I'll call you back and let you know what happens."

Chris, whoever he was, hung up the phone. He never called back.

One of the jurors had been late arriving, which had put things a bit behind schedule, but at ten past nine the sheriff's officer came out to tell us we could enter the courtroom. Nate and I got up and walked in, followed a minute later by the prosecutor. The judge then stuck her head into the courtroom and asked if we were ready to proceed; we were. She told the officers to "line up" the jury, which was assembled in the jury room. Within five minutes, the jurors were walking single file into the courtroom. As they proceeded past us, none of them made any eye contact with the prosecutor, with me, or with Nate. Seeing them lined up like that, I wondered to myself if they were the rescue party or the execution squad. Only time would tell.

Once the jurors took their seats, we heard a crisp knock from the back door that led from the judge's chambers to the courtroom. A sheriff's officer shouted "All rise," and we sprang to our feet. Through the door walked the judge, who quickly took the bench. She greeted everyone and then asked the prosecutor if she was ready to give an opening. The prosecutor rose from her chair and began,

"Your Honor, Mr. Hartmann, Ladies and Gentlemen of the Jury."
Her opening lasted a little over 10 minutes. The length was right on,
but I didn't think it was that convincing. She went over the facts of
the case and the burden of proof (thank you for that one). She didn't
come up with any surprises and most importantly, she really couldn't
explain the horrendous identification by the victim. When she sat
down, I was feeling even more confident.

"Mr. Hartmann, do you wish to give an opening?" the judge
inquired. The reason she asked is because I had a choice, since the
burden is on the State. In theory, I could sit and do nothing. I didn't
have to give an opening. I didn't have to cross-examine witnesses,
and I didn't have to give a summation. My only requirements,
according to the Rehnquist Court, were to stay (pretty) sober and to
stay (semi) awake during trial. In reality, of course, had I not given
an opening my client would have fired me on the spot, and I have
never heard of a lawyer opting not to give an opening.

I stood up and informed the court that I wished to address the
jury. My opening lasted 15 minutes. I set the stage for the case, how
Nate was just sitting on a bench minding his own business, going to
work, when his entire world fell apart. I focused on the poor investigation. I focused on the poor identification. I focused on reasonable doubt. Finally, I focused on Nate. This really was one of the
cases where a juror could relate to the defendant. The opening went
very well. I finished with, "And when you have listened to all of the
evidence and listened to the judge's instructions, the evidence is
going to clearly indicate that my client is innocent, and I submit that
you will return a verdict of not guilty because he is, in fact, innocent." I felt that I had really connected with the jury.

The State called its first witness to the stand, the detective who conducted the investigation. I wasn't impressed with his investigation,

and by the time he was through, I wasn't impressed with his testimony. He had an air about him that now that he worked for the Feds, he was too important for this rinky-dink robbery shit. Just a few years before, he was investigating "smash and grab" car burglaries at the local strip mall; now he was working for Homeland Security, and he acted like Jack Bauer. The ex-detective appeared bored on direct, but after I started taking some shots at him, he quickly bristled, as if to say, "How dare you doubt me?" I wanted to give the jury the impression that he was somebody who was just going through the motions, somebody who just wanted to clear one more file off his desk. After crossing him for over half an hour, I think I was successful.

You have to be careful how you cross-examine witnesses; you can't just go in with guns blazing for all of them. Some witnesses, especially victims, you have to treat with kid gloves. Some witnesses who are not central to the case can be treated in a matter-of-fact manner. But with police officers, especially when you think they made a mistake, or worse—when you think they're not telling the truth—you can go after them pretty hard. They are law enforcement professionals and should expect such treatment. Moreover, a jury expects that the "boys in blue" can handle it.

Cross-examination is one area of the law where you really do get better with practice. Once you start doing it on a regular basis, you get a feel for what questions to ask and how to ask them. That being said, you can do an adequate job even during your first trial if you heed the following advice.

The characteristics of a successful cross-examiner are very similar to the characteristics of a successful politician. A successful politician spends all his waking hours thinking of ways to screw his opponent. It is the same with a successful cross-examiner. You have to spend time thinking about what line of questioning to follow. If there is a key witness you have to hurt on the stand, think constantly about different possible questions to ask that witness, and when something pops into your head, write it down. I like to take yellow stickies, scribble notes on them, and put them in my wallet. Before a big case, I will have my wallet filled with a dozen stickies, all with different lines of questioning.

Once you have formulated the tack you will take with questioning, write your questions out. This is imperative. When I have an important witness, I type out all the questions I intend to ask him. Unless you are *extremely* talented and experienced, you cannot "wing" a good cross-examination. In the heat of the cross-examination, you will forget an important line of questioning. You will finish your cross, and the witness will be excused. As he is walking out the door, it will suddenly hit you, "Oh, no! I forgot to ask him about the lighting, which he'd described as 'poor' in his original statement!" Don't let this happen to you. Write out your cross-examination and put the script in your trial notebook. And by the way, if there are good facts, repeat them to the witness. If the lighting was poor, whenever you refer to the lighting in cross-examination, it is not "the lighting," it is "the *poor* lighting." You have been living with this case for a couple of weeks, the jury hasn't. You know all the ins and outs of the case, the jury doesn't. Don't be coy, be blunt. Repetition is a very good thing.

Next, there is the old saying that you should never ask a question on cross-examination that you don't know the answer to. There is a reason why you learn this rule the first day of law school: It is true. If you don't know what answer the witness will give, don't ask the question. It's that simple. A friend was trying a multi-defendant bank robbery case in Federal Court. A teller took the stand and identified a number of the defendants. After a round of questioning, the lawyer for a defendant who was not identified asked the teller, "Do you recognize anyone else who committed the robbery?" The teller looked around, pointed at his client, and said, "Yes, he was there, too." At this point, the lawyer should have whipped out his checkbook and cut the client a check for the full amount of his fee. By asking one incredibly stupid question, he had probably just put his client away for 20 years.

Along the same line, you are always better off asking one question too few than one question too many. You have a witness on the stand and you are scoring a lot of points with good questions. Resist the temptation to go for the throat with that one final question. It rarely pays off and you might get burned.

Finally, only ask leading questions. Ideally, the witness should answer only "yes," with an occasional "no." You are telling what happened and the witness is agreeing with you. Never let the witness elaborate on cross. That is what direct is for. Never ask open-ended questions. And never, ever ask the witness their opinion—it will almost always backfire. For instance, if you have a drug case and the issue is whether the defendant was in possession of the drugs for personal use or to distribute, don't ask the police officer, "Now officer, don't these facts suggest the heroin was for my client's personal use?" If you ask that question, you will get bent over; police officers aren't stupid. Get the facts you want from the witness and you can argue the conclusion to the jury in summation.

In Nate's case, after the detective-turned-Fed had testified, the prosecutor called two witnesses. One was the first police officer at the scene. He didn't hurt us. In fact, he helped us because he stated that the victim—the cashier—was very upset when he arrived. The second was another officer peripherally involved in the investigation. His testimony was inconsequential.

The final witness for the State was the cashier, and she was called right after the lunch break. I had never seen her before, and when she walked in, I was a little surprised. Like a bride in an Appalachian shotgun wedding, she was clearly pregnant, probably seven or eight months along. This wasn't good; the jury was going to feel protective of her and give her the benefit of any doubt. During cross-examination, I would be treading on thin ice. As soon as the prosecutor began questioning her, I realized it was worse than I'd first imagined. The witness was extremely timid, and as I glanced over at the jury from time to time, I could tell they were sympathetic. Her testimony, at least, brought no surprises. She went over what happened and identified Nate as the culprit. She was done in half an hour.

I knew I would have to attack this witness's credibility immediately, and I began by focusing on the weakest part of her testimony, concerning the perpetrator's height. I went through all of the basics with her: It happened very quickly, you were nervous, you were focusing on the knife, etc. Then I stood up and continued the questioning more or less as follows.

"Tell me, how tall do you think I am?"

"About six feet tall," she answered.

I am five foot ten on a good day, and while personally I was starting to like this witness, it was my job to attack her credibility. Critical to my case was the fact that she'd described the assailant as less than six feet tall, making him shorter than I am.

"Now, the man who robbed you was about my height?"

"Yes," she responded.

Perfect, I thought to myself, she is falling into the trap. Not that setting the trap demonstrated any great legal prowess. To be honest, as an experienced defense attorney going up against a pregnant 20-year-old, I felt like a big game hunter packing an elephant gun for tracking a koala bear, but it was my job. Next, I had Nate stand up. I could physically feel his tension as he rose and towered over me.

"What is the height of the man standing next to me?"

"He is probably seven feet tall."

"So you think this man is seven feet tall."

"Yes."

"So this seven-foot-tall man is the same height as Wilt Chamberlain?"

"Who is Wilt Chamberlain?"

"It doesn't matter. Now, the robber was less than six feet tall, correct?"

"Yes."

"He was slightly shorter than I am."

"About the same height."

"And this man standing next to me is clearly much taller than I am?"

"Yes."

"According to your testimony, he is a foot taller than me."

"Yes."

The cross-examination continued in that vein for several minutes. When we were done, I was feeling very, very confident. The State rested, and thus ended the first day of trial.

Nate and I left the courtroom and headed outside. At the bottom of the courthouse stairs, we had a brief conversation about how things were progressing. I felt good, but my client was nervous. We briefly spoke about his testifying. All along, I had intended to have him take the stand. But now, I wasn't so certain it was the right

move. Right now, the case was all about the sloppy investigation
and the terrible identification. Right now, if the jury went into deliberation, my gut told me they would return a verdict of not guilty. If
Nate testified, the case might become about him and whether he
was lying and not about the fact that the robber had grown over a
foot in three years. I explained this all to Nate and looked him right
into his drawn eyes and asked, "Do you want to testify?" He immediately answered, "Yes, I do."

I responded with a grin, "All right, baby, let's roll!" and slapped
him lightly on his left arm. For one of the few times since I'd met
him, a slight smile crossed Nate's face.

The next day broke with the sun behind the clouds. It would
remain overcast all day. As always, I awoke around 6:00 AM and
was out of the house by 8:15 and at the courthouse half an hour
later. To my surprise, Nate wasn't there. I waited for about five minutes and still no client. This was unusual, and I called him on his
cell. He answered and said he was right around the corner. I went
outside and walked up to two legal secretaries I knew who were
partaking of their morning cigarettes. We greeted each other and
exchanged pleasantries. Soon I saw Nate coming up South Broad
Street. I told the women to have a nice day and went to meet him.

I walked up to my client and said, "Nate, it's showtime. Are you
ready to do this?" He answered in a serious tone of voice, "Yes, Mr.
Hartmann, I am. I have been waiting for this day for over three long
years."

Together, we went inside, walked into court, and sat down. The
prosecutor was already there, and I informed her that my client
would be testifying. A short time later, the judge stuck her head outside her door and asked us if we had to discuss anything before the
jury came in. I told her that Nathaniel would be taking the stand.

"All right," she said, "I better get outta here." Soon she came out
with her robes on and sat down. She asked Nate to rise and then
asked me if she could address my client, a request to which I con-
sented. The judge told Nate that he had an absolute right not to testify and that fact could not be used against him. She then inquired
if he had any questions for her or for me. Nate said he did not. The
judge then inquired of my client, "Do you wish to testify?" He
responded in a loud voice, "I do."

"Very well," the judge said, "bring in the jury."

Nate's testimony went well. We had prepared extensively and, on
direct, he carefully went through his side of the story. On cross, he
by and large kept his cool, and I didn't feel the prosecutor scored
any points. When the judge asked me if I had any re-direct, I
thought for a second before replying, "No, Your Honor." During
Nate's testimony, I had looked over at the jury, and they seemed to
be paying attention. You can sometimes tell that jurors don't believe
a witness if they don't look at him, if they shake their heads slightly,
or if they cover their mouths with their hands. I saw none of this
negative body language from any juror during Nate's testimony.
They had listened attentively and quietly, and I couldn't have asked
for anything more. When the judge told Nate he was excused and he
got up and walked over to the defense table and sat down, I felt that
his testimony had only helped his case.

The judge then asked me if I had any other witnesses. I
responded that I did not and then said "The defense rests." The
judge announced, "Ladies and Gentlemen, the State and the
Defense have rested. You will have your mid-morning break and
then return for summations." The jury got up and marched past us
to the door. They looked serious, much more serious than the day

before. They knew that soon they would have to make an important decision that would have a profound impact on a person's life.

Summations are the easiest part of the case. Once you have spent time preparing your case and then living and breathing a trial, giving a well-thought-out summation with little practice is relatively easy. You will have no problem speaking for a half-hour from a page of notes. Unfortunately, while summations are the simplest part of the case, they are also the least important. Most jurors have made up their minds and what you say won't change anything.

I do not consider myself an exceptional public speaker. I am probably a little better than most, but I'm no spellbinder. On that day in May, however, I was on fire. I think it was my most impassioned, moving summation ever. And the jury loved it. They were paying attention, and they were nodding in approval. Usually when you give a summation, half the jurors seem to be nodding off and the other half have that starry-eyed look. Not today. After bringing it for twenty minutes, I reached my crescendo and exclaimed:

"We can go through our entire lives and never have the opportunity to right a wrong. But you will have that opportunity today. Each one of you will be able to right the wrong that happened three years ago, when an innocent man was charged with a crime he did not commit. Soon, 12 of you will go into that jury room, and there you can review the facts. There you can render a verdict of not guilty. There you can end this terrible injustice that has happened to my client. There, you can right this wrong!"

And with that I closed.

The prosecutor gave her summation but it didn't really matter. Nothing she could say or do would change a thing. I had a feeling that the jurors had already made up their minds.

After summations, we had a short break. Nate appeared nervous but I reassured him as best I could. We sat there talking about his testimony and the summations. At this point, he thanked me for the job I had done and said that whatever the verdict, he knew I had given it my all. I appreciated his words and told him so. We shook hands, and I was taken aback by his sweaty grip. I could only imagine what he was going through.

We went back into the courtroom, the jury assembled, and the judge came out to give the jury charge. The charge lasted about 45 minutes. I half paid attention as I doodled on my yellow notepad, drawing three dimensional boxes and smiley faces with glasses. Maybe the marks are a map of my psyche. Maybe they only mean I am bored, but I have been drawing the same doodles since high school. And if my inane doodles do mean that I am crazy, well that's only par for the course.

The judge finished the jury charge by saying, "And now, ladies and gentlemen, the case is in your hands, but first we have to select the two alternate jurors." It always seems that the best jurors are made the alternates, but not in this case. Twelve jurors with whom I was happy were selected and the Princeton University professor was made the foreman. Things were looking good.

I walked outside with my client, and we sat down on a cool marble bench. It was clear that he didn't want to talk so I just sat there, pulled out another file and my calendar, did some work, and made a few calls. I waited 45 minutes and went back to the judge's chambers. A prosecutor with whom I had another case was waiting for me to see the judge in that matter. We announced to the judge's secretary that we were ready to see her, and two minutes later we were motioned into the judge's office. We walked in, sat down, and started to talk.

The judge really didn't have a lot to do at the time so our talk moved on to various other topics. About half an hour into our conversation, there was a knock and a sheriff's officer walked in. He said, "We have a verdict." The judge thanked the officer then turned to me and offered her congratulations.

It is a general misconception that juries returning with a quick verdict usually vote to convict. This is incorrect. Quick verdicts are usually not guilty verdicts. The reason for this is that if a jury is going to convict, they want to make certain they are making the right decision. Therefore, they will break at the end of the day to at least mull their decision overnight. Guilty verdicts often come back about one hour into the second day of deliberation. If a jury is going to find a person not guilty, on the other hand, then why drag things out? Get it over with. Of course, this is just a general rule. In the third trial I ever did (not surprisingly in Somerset County), my client was actually found guilty in less time than it takes a group of stoners to go through a tray of Tater Tots. No joking, within 16 minutes the jury was coming back into the courtroom, all stone-faced and sullen. That was one hanging jury. And to make matters worse, they had to read a 12-page transcript during deliberation. I was working for Roger Daley at the time and when I told him about my complete ignominy, he joked that an issue for appeal was that the jury could not have possibly deliberated.

I went to the courthouse entrance and called for Nate. He was just where I had left him; this time his legs were apart, and he was sitting bent over with his hands clasped in front of him as if in prayer. He looked up at me with worried eyes, and I told him, "The jury has a verdict." We went into the courtroom and, for the last time, took our seats at counsel table and waited. It took about 10 minutes to get everyone in, including an extra sheriff's officer. For me, those 10 minutes seemed like an hour. For Nate, they must have seemed like an eternity. Finally, there was a knock on the courtroom door and the officer announced "Jury entering." For the first and only time during the trial, I stood for the 12 jurors as they walked single file into the courtroom. I was nervous. What if the unthinkable happened and Nate was found guilty? How would he deal with it?

I have had my fair share of guilty verdicts, and my experience has been that the defendant almost always takes his or her verdict stoically. It impresses me how these people, many of whom who have exhibited very little self control during their entire life, can stand there dispassionately, like a Buddhist monk, as their life evaporates before them.

Now, family members—that's a different story. Brothers, cousins, sisters, and girlfriends have been known to start melees when a loved one goes down in flames. I was once in Middlesex County Court and heard a ruckus emanating from a courtroom. Some "Traveler" (aka "Tinker" or "Irish Gypsy") had just been convicted of a fourth degree offense. The ensuing Donnybrook between the little Irish people and the sheriff's officers resembled a pub in South Boston at closing time on St. Patrick's Day. All that was missing was the Guinness and the Jameson's, and the Pogues blaring on the jukebox.

After a verdict has been reached, you can almost always tell from the demeanor of the jurors as they enter the courtroom what their verdict will be. When they reach a verdict of not guilty, it is as if a weight has been lifted from their shoulders. They are smiling. As they walk by the defense table, one or two of them may even look directly at the defendant with a faint smile. However, if the jurors walk in stone-faced or frowning and staring straight ahead, then you are coming in second.

Nate's jury walked in and ... they were smiling! There was even light banter among two or three of them. As they walked by, many were doing their best to suppress a smile. A couple cast a quick glance at Nate. The professor even gave me a wink (now *that* was a first). Within a minute, they were in the jury box, positioned in front of their seats. Looking at them standing there, well, "it was a beautiful thing" as my Italian friends from Chambersburg might say.

The judge entered the courtroom and told everyone to sit with the exception of the foreman, who remained standing with a sheet of paper in his hand. The clerk addressed the foreman.

"Mr. Foreman, have you reached a verdict?" the clerk asked.

"Yes," replied the foreman.

"And is that verdict unanimous?"

"Yes."

"And how do you find in regards to count one, robbery in the first degree, guilty or not guilty?"

"Not guilty."

Nate stood there, and for the only time since I knew him, he showed emotion. With his right hand, he made a barely perceptible fist pump.

After the verdict, the judge had the jury pooled. They were asked individually if they agreed with the verdict. They did. Then they were thanked by the judge and told something along the lines that the system wouldn't work if there weren't people willing to serve on juries. They were then excused. This time as they left single file, everyone smiled at Nate. A few even said congratulations. Nate thanked them all in his quiet voice. As the last juror left, the judge turned to the defense table and said, "Mr. Smith, you are free to go." That sounded almost as sweet as hearing the verdict.

I turned to my client, shook his sweaty hand again, looked up at him, and said, "Thank God that's over." When he responded, "Yes, thank God, and thank you, Mr. Hartmann," I thought it was about the nicest thing a client had ever said to me. It's funny, I have had a number of cases where we do well in trial and family members thank God and Jesus, acting like I had nothing to do with it. But when a client is on the business end of a guilty verdict, it's all me.

I asked Nate to wait outside for me. Then I walked over to the prosecutor and shook her hand, telling her she did a good job. She chuckled and told me she would get me next time (she did). County prosecutors are often forced to try weak cases and, to their credit, they usually take losing in stride. U.S. Attorneys on the other hand, if they lose too many cases (too many being one), will find themselves prosecuting motor vehicle violations on an army base outside of Nome, Alaska.

I loaded up the sarcophagus and headed out. After successfully completing a case, you would think I'd be relaxed and overjoyed. In actuality, I felt a little blue. I had put so much effort into the case and invested so much time that now, having seen it through, in a strange way I was feeling melancholy.

Nate was waiting for me at the bottom of the courthouse steps. He gave me a half-cocked grin and thanked me again. I said it was my pleasure and told him to call if I could do anything for him in the future. I then added, "Nate, I have done approximately 50 jury trials, and you are the only client whose innocence I never doubted." Intentionally hesitating, I gave him my best wry smile and said, "Nate, you *are* innocent—right?"

My client broke into a grin from ear to ear and started to laugh. "Yes, John," he said at last, "I am innocent."

Nate turned away and headed down South Broad Street. Watching
as he strode toward the center of the city, his loose arms swinging
freely at this side, I savored the moment. My thoughts took me back
to something that Roger Daley said when I first joined him years earlier in that small office in New Brunswick. He told me that William
Blackstone, in his seminal work, *Commentaries on English Law*,
wrote, "It is better that ten guilty people escape than one innocent
suffer." It was a great quote. Now, a cynic might say that I like the
quote because I am a defense attorney, and they would be partially
right in saying so. However, think of the alternative—think of what
the Khmer Rouge leader, Pol Pot, is purported to have said: "It is
better that ten innocent men suffer than one guilty man escape."
History has demonstrated in abundance that while people may commit crimes, governments commit atrocities. By vigorously defending the rights of individuals, we keep in check the excesses of the
government which, if allowed to grow unbridled, would consume us
all. This is the reason I chose to become a criminal defense attorney.

It was a travesty that Nathaniel Smith spent over three years in
jail. But in a strange way, the result was a justification of our system. In the end, the system worked. An appellate court got it right
and reversed my client's conviction. And then a jury of his peers
exonerated him. We muddled our way through, but eventually justice was done. I continued to think to myself, "Law school in
Newark, taking the bar twice, opening my practice, the late nights,
the countless hours over the years visiting defendants in jail and
prison, the crazy clients, it was all worth it just to have helped right
one terrible wrong."

My moment of internal reflection was suddenly broken by a loud
and familiar voice. "How are you doing, Mr. Hartmann?" I turned
around to see a former client by the name of Edward Wilson just

crossing the street toward me. Wilson and a friend had been busted for selling their prescription drugs out of a bodega a year earlier. He was in his late fifties and his co-defendant was well into his sixties. They were both facing time, if for no other reason than neither had led a particularly virtuous life before coming up with the drug scheme. However, the prosecutor took one look at the "geriatric crew" during arraignment and gave them probation on the spot. He figured that no jury was going to convict a couple of seniors for slinging their medications. We were coming out of a recession, after all, and times were tough.

En route to the new courthouse to report to probation, Wilson had taken a detour in my direction. Approaching me he said cheerfully, "Mr. Hartmann, haven't seen you in a minute." (Translation: "I haven't seen you in awhile.") "You the man, Mr. Hartmann," he continued, and I assumed at this point he had heard about Nate and was going to congratulate me. I was wrong. My erstwhile client said, "But Mr. Hartmann, man, you were too heavy on my pockets!" (Translation: "You charged me too much!")

I was about to remind him that while I may have been heavy, he remained light, to the tune of $500. I caught myself in mid-thought and instead just said, "Mr. Wilson, it's great to see you again."

"What are you up to, Mr. Hartmann?" he asked in a friendly voice.

"I'm on my way to the workhouse to visit a new client. He's got a pretty serious charge, and he swears on a stack of Bibles he didn't do it."

"Do you think he's innocent?" Wilson asked.

After thinking about it for a moment, I said, "You know what, Mr. Wilson? I still don't much care."

Edward Wilson let out a good-natured chuckle. "Thank God, you don't, Mr. Hartmann. Thank God, you don't!"

ABOUT THE AUTHOR

John W. Hartmann is an attorney with a small practice in West Windsor, New Jersey. He is married and has two children. He has written one other book, *The American Partisan: Henry Lee and the Struggle for Independence, 1776–1780*, a well-researched and well-written work that few people read and even fewer purchased.

John is currently working on his first novel.